KNIT
the Alphabet

Claire Garland

David and Charles

CONTENTS

WELCOME

What could be sweeter to give as a gift than a homemade, hand-knitted letter, a bundle of little letters that spell out someone's name, or a loving word or phrase for a special person? The knitted letters in this book allow you to do just that, and more. Letters used as objet d'art are seen in many magazines and blogs and this idea led me to create medium-sized letters too, which can be used to adorn walls and shelves. I then created even larger letters, which are perfect for floppy, cuddly cushions and individual pillows.

There is plenty of scope here for names and initials, words and phrases for celebrations and occasions such as Christmas, weddings and birthdays. You are sure to come up with many ideas to have fun with the designs, for example, imagine a rug made up from the letters R U G, all joined together!

Each letter gives the yarn and needle requirements, plus the finished sizes and gauge (tension). There are also suggestions on the type and colour of yarn to use for each of the sizes, although I hope that this book will encourage you to experiment with using different yarn types, colours and patterns, so that each letter will become as individual as the person for whom it is intended.

I have designed each letter to be knitted as one piece, with a cast on method similar to that in the making of a toe in a sock. The letters are then knitted in the round. For those new to knitting, all the techniques you need are at the back of the book, along with an abbreviation list and advice on finishing off and staging the letters. Happy knitting!

Claire Garland

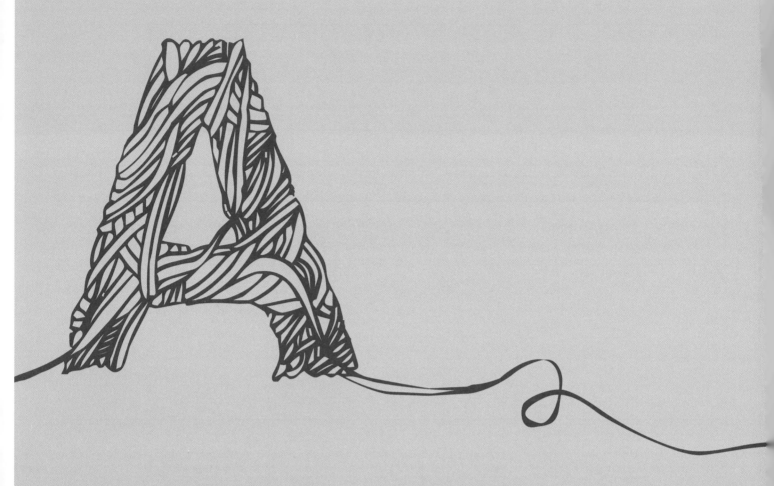

YOU WILL NEED

SMALL
35yds (32m) of fingering-weight (4ply) yarn
1 set of 5 dpns size 1 (2.5mm)
2 sets of size 1 (2.5mm) circular needles

MEDIUM
57yds (52m) of worsted weight (Aran) yarn
1 set of 5 dpns size 8 (5mm)
2 sets of size 8 (5mm) circular needles

LARGE
101yds (92m) of bulky weight (chunky) yarn
1 set of 5 dpns size 15 (10mm)
2 sets of size 15 (10mm) circular needles

NOTIONS
Blunt-ended tapestry needle
Toy filling
Row counter

GAUGE (TENSION)
SMALL 30 sts x 39 rows to 4in (10cm) over st st
MEDIUM 18 sts x 25 rows to 4in (10cm) over st st
LARGE 7.5 sts x 10 rows to 4in (10cm) over st st

FINISHED SIZE (APPROX)
SMALL 6in x 5in (15cm x 13cm)
MEDIUM 9¾in x 7in (24cm x 18cm)
LARGE 15¾in x 13¾in (40cm x 35cm)
(For the largest size it may be easier to work directly onto circular needles)

YARN CHOICES

Small: Rowan Pure Wool 4ply Shale 402
Medium: Rowan Pure Wool Aran Splash 701
Large: Rowan Big Wool Steel 052 and Reseda 069

GET KNITTING

Left side of letter

Using simple sock cast on method (see Techniques), cast on 28 sts.

Rnd 1 K28.

Divide sts equally between 2 circular ndls (14 sts on each), with yarn at tip of RH ndl. Have LH sts at top of ndl to be worked. PM.

Rnds 2–4 K28.

Rnd 5 (dec) Skpo, k2tog, k6, skpo, k2tog, skpo, k2tog, k6, skpo, k2tog. (20 sts)

Rnd 6 K20.

Rnd 7 (dec) Skpo, k2tog, k2, skpo, k2tog, skpo, k2tog, k2, skpo, k2tog. (12 sts)

Rnd 8 K12.

Rnd 9 K1, kfb, k1, k2tog, k1, k1, skpo, k1, kfb, k1.

Rep last 2 rnds 5 times ending at back of left side of letter.

Cut yarn and sl two sets of sts onto 2 dpns and set aside.

Right side of letter

Using simple sock cast on method, cast on 38 sts.

Rnd 1 K38.

Divide sts equally between 2 circular ndls (19 sts on each ndl), with yarn at tip of RH ndl – have LH sts at top of ndl to be worked. PM.

Rnds 2–4 K38.

Rnd 5 (dec) Skpo, k2tog, k11, skpo, k2tog, skpo, k2tog, k11, skpo, k2tog. (30 sts)

Rnd 6 K30.

Rnd 7 (dec) Skpo, k2tog, k7, skpo, k2tog, skpo, k2tog, k7, skpo, k2tog. (22 sts)

Rnd 8 K22.

Rnd 9 K1, skpo, k6, kfb, k1, k1, kfb, k6, k2tog, k1.

Rep last 2 rnds 5 times.

Join sides together

Rnd 20 K11 sts from front of RHS, cast on 13 sts onto same ndl using backward loop method, k6 from front of LHS, slide rem 6 sts onto second circular ndl - (back sts of RHS will be facing), k these 6 sts, cast on 13 sts using backward loop method, k11 from back RHS. (60 sts – 30 sts on each ndl).

Cont in rnds keeping tension tight across joins to avoid gaps and taking care not to twist cast on sts.

Rnd 21 (dec) K1, skpo, k24, k2tog, k1, k1, skpo, k24, k2tog, k1. (56 sts)

Rnd 22 K56.

Rnd 23 (dec) K1, skpo, k22, k2tog, k1, k1, skpo, k22, k2tog, k1. (52 sts)

Rnd 24 K52.

Rnd 25 (dec) K1, skpo, k20, k2tog, k1, k1, skpo, k20, k2tog, k1. (48 sts)

Rnd 26 K48.

Rnd 27 (dec) K1, skpo, k18, k2tog, k1, k1, skpo, k18, k2tog, k1. (44 sts)

Rnd 28 K44.

Rnd 29 (dec) K1, skpo, k16, k2tog, k1, k1, skpo, k16, k2tog, k1. (40 sts)

Rnd 30 (dec) K8, kfb, k1, bind (cast) off 5 sts, kfb, k3, k3, kfb, k1, bind (cast) off 5 sts, kfb, k8.

Cont with right side sts only as folls:

Rnd 31 K1, skpo, k6, kfb, k1, sl next 6 sts from left side onto a dpn, sl next 6 sts from left back onto another dpn. Cont with rem 11 sts from RHS shaping as folls: k1, kfb, k6, k2tog, k1.

Rnd 32 K22.

Rnd 33 K1, skpo, k6, kfb, k1, k1, kfb, k6, k2tog, k1.

Rep last 2 rnds 7 times so ending at back of RHS of letter. Cut yarn.

Rejoin yarn to 6 sts at front of LHS – working with dpns or circulars, cont, shaping as folls:

Rnd 31 K1, kfb, k1, k2tog, k1, k1, skpo, k1, kfb, k1. Join in the rnd.

Rnd 32 K12.

Rep last 2 rnds 7 times.

Rnd 47 K1, kfb, k1, k2tog, k1, k1, skpo, k1, kfb, k1. Cut yarn.

Join sides for apex

Rnd 48 Rejoin yarn k11 from front of RHS, k6 from front of LHS onto same ndl, slide next 6 sts from back of LHS to join 11 sts from back of RHS and k across onto other ndl. (34 sts – 17sts on each ndl)

Rnd 49 (dec) K1, skpo, k11, k2tog, k1, k1, skpo, k11, k2tog, k1. (30 sts)

Rnd 50 K30.

Rnd 51 (dec) K1, skpo, k9, k2tog, k1, k1, skpo, k9, k2tog, k1. (26 sts)

Rnd 52 K26.

Rnd 53 (dec) K1, skpo, k7, k2tog, k1, k1, skpo, k7, k2tog, k1. (22 sts)

Rnd 54 K22.

Rnd 55 (dec) K1, skpo, k5, k2tog, k1, k1, skpo, k5, k2tog, k1. (18 sts)

Rnd 56 K18.

Rnd 57 (dec) K1, skpo, k3, k2tog, k1, k1, skpo, k3, k2tog, k1. (14 sts)

Rnd 58 K14.

Rnd 59 (dec) K1, skpo, k1, k2tog, k1, k1, skpo, k1, k2tog, k1. (10 sts)

Rnd 60 (dec) Skpo, k1, k2tog, skpo, k1, k2tog. (6 sts)

Cut yarn, thread end through rem 6 sts, pull up tight to close gap and weave in end to secure.

TO FINISH OFF

Stuff letter firmly and evenly through openings. Close seams with mattress stitch. Weave in tail ends.

YOU WILL NEED

SMALL
55yds (50m) of fingering-weight (4ply) yarn
1 set of 5 dpns size 1 (2.5mm)
2 sets of size 1 (2.5mm) circular needles

MEDIUM
104yds (95m) of worsted weight (Aran) yarn
1 set of 5 dpns size 8 (5mm)
2 sets of size 8 (5mm) circular needles

LARGE
132yds (120m) of bulky weight (chunky) yarn
1 set of 5 dpns size 15 (10mm)
2 sets of size 15 (10mm) circular needles

NOTIONS
Blunt-ended tapestry needle
Toy filling
Row counter

GAUGE (TENSION)
SMALL 30 sts x 39 rows to 4in (10cm) over st st
MEDIUM 18 sts x 25 rows to 4in (10cm) over st st
LARGE 7.5 sts x 10 rows to 4in (10cm) over st st

FINISHED SIZE (APPROX)
SMALL 5¼in x 4¼in (13.5cm x 11cm)
MEDIUM 9½in x 7in (24cm x 18cm)
LARGE 15¾in x 13¾in (40cm x 35cm)

YARN CHOICES

Small: Rowan Pure Wool 4ply Eau de Nil 450
Medium: Rowan Pure Wool Aran Burnt 700
Large: (not shown) Rowan Big Wool Lipstick 063

GET KNITTING

For Small and Medium letters you may need to wind off two separate balls for working the two sides.

Beginning at the bottom of letter working with RS facing work as folls:

Using simple sock cast on method (see Techniques), cast on 52 sts, (26 sts on each ndl).

Rnd 1 K52.

Divide sts equally between 2 circular ndls (26 sts on each ndl), with yarn at tip of RH ndl – have LH sts at top of ndl to be worked. PM.

Rnd 2 (inc) K1, kfb, k24, k24, kfb, k1. (54 sts)

Rnd 3 (dec) Kfb, k21, skpo, k2tog, k1, k1, skpo, k2tog, k21, kfb. (52 sts)

Rnd 4 (inc) K1, kfb, k24, k24, kfb, k1. (54 sts)

Rnd 5 (dec) Kfb, k21, skpo, k2tog, k1, k1, skpo, k2tog, k21, kfb. (52 sts)

Rep last 2 rnds once.

Rnd 8 (inc) K1, kfb, k24, k24, kfb, k1. (54 sts)

Divide straight side from curved side

Rnd 9 K1, kfb, k6, k2tog, bind (cast) off 6 sts, k10, k11 bind (cast) off 7 sts, k6, kfb, k1.

Bottom curve

Rnd 10 K10, sl next 11 sts off circular ndl and onto a dpn and set aside, sl next 11 sts off circular ndl and onto another dpn and set aside, k10 for back of curved side, working on

these 20 sts only join in rnd and cont as folls:

Rnd 11 (inc) K1, kfb, k8, k8, kfb, k1. (22 sts)

Rnds 12 & 13 K22.

Rnd 14 K1, kfb, k6, k2tog, k1, k1, skpo, k6, kfb, k1.

Rnds 15–21 K22.

Rnd 22 K1, skpo, k6, kfb, k1, k1, kfb, k6, k2tog, k1.

Rnds 23 & 24 K22.

Rnd 25 (dec) K1, skpo, k8, k8, k2tog, k1.

Rnd 26 K20.

Set aside these 20 sts and return to 22 sts on dpns for straight side using other end of yarn (or a fresh ball).

Straight side

With RS facing and with dpns (or spare circulars) rejoin yarn to inner edge and cont as folls:

Rnd 9 K22.

Join in the rnd.

Rep last rnd 17 times. Cut yarn.

Join curved side with straight side

With RS facing cont as folls:

Rnd 27 (inc) K1, skpo, k5, kfb, k1, backward loop cast on 4 sts, k across first set of 11 sts from straight side – (25 sts on ndl), sl 2nd set of 11 sts from straight side onto second circular ndl then k across, backward loop cast on 4 sts, then work across

rem sts from curved side as folls: k1, kfb, k5, k2tog, k1 (25 sts on second circular). Join in the rnd.

Rnd 28 K50.

Rnd 29 (dec) K1, skpo, k22, k22, k2tog, k1. (48 sts)

Rnd 30 K48.

Rnd 31 (dec) K1, skpo, k21, k21, k2tog, k1. (46 sts)

Rnd 32 K46.

Rnd 33 (inc) K1, kfb, k21, k21, kfb, k1. (48 sts)

Rnd 34 K48.

Add top curve

Rnd 35 (dec) K1, kfb, k7, bind (cast) off 4 sts, k10, k11, bind (cast) off 4 sts, k6, kfb, k1.

Rnd 36 K10, sl next 11 sts off circular ndl and onto a dpn and set aside, sl next 11 sts off circular and onto another dpn and set aside, k10 for back of curved side and cont on these 20 sts as folls:

Rnd 37 (inc) K1, kfb, k8, k8, kfb, k1. (22 sts)

Rnds 38 & 39 K22.

Rnd 40 K1, kfb, k6, k2tog, k1, k1, skpo, k6, kfb, k1.

Rnds 41–47 K22.

Rnd 48 K1, skpo, k6, kfb, k1, k1, kfb, k6, k2tog, k1.

Rnds 49 & 50 K22.

Rnd 51 (dec) K1, skpo, k8, k8, k2tog, k1.

Rnd 52 K20.

Set aside these 20 sts and return to 22 sts on dpns for straight side using other end of yarn (or other ball).

Straight side

Rejoin yarn to 22 sts from LH side joining yarn to sts just after bind (cast) off – working with dpns (or spare circulars), cont as folls:

Rnd 36 K22. Join in the rnd.

Rep last rnd 16 times. Cut yarn.

Join curved side with straight side

With RS facing return to curved side and cont as folls:

Rnd 53 (inc) K1, skpo, k5, kfb, k1, backward loop cast on 4 sts, k across first set of 11 sts from straight side – all onto one ndl. Sl 2nd set of 11 sts from straight side onto other circular ndl and then k across them, backward loop cast on 4 sts, then work across rem sts from curved side shaping as folls: k1, kfb, k5, k2tog, k1. (50 sts)

Rnd 54 (inc) K23, kfb, k1, k1, kfb, k23. (52 sts)

Rnd 55 (inc) Skpo, k22, m1, k1, kfb, kfb, k1, m1, k22, k2tog. (54 sts)

Rnd 56 (dec) K1, skpo, k24, k24, k2tog, k1. (52 sts)

Rnd 57 (inc) Skpo, k22, m1, k1, kfb, kfb, k1, m1, k22, k2 tog. (54 sts)

Rnd 58 K1, skpo, k24, k24, k2tog, k1. (52 sts)

Rnd 59 Skpo, k22, m1, k1, kfb, kfb, k1, m1, k22, k2tog. (54 sts)

Rnd 60 K1, skpo, k24, k24, k2tog, k1. (52 sts)

Cut yarn leaving a tail end 6 times the length of the sts on one needle.

TO FINISH OFF

Hold 2 sets of 26 sts parallel in your left hand. Thread cut yarn end with a sewing needle then work Kitchener stitch (see Techniques) to close the seam neatly.

Stuff the letter firmly and evenly through the openings. Close the opening with mattress stitch. Weave in tail ends.

YOU WILL NEED

SMALL
18½yds (17m) of fingering-weight (4ply) yarn
1 set of 5 dpns size 1 (2.5mm)
2 sets of size 1 (2.5mm) circular needles

MEDIUM
46yds (42m) of worsted weight (Aran) yarn
1 set of 5 dpns size 8 (5mm)
2 sets of size 8 (5mm) circular needles

LARGE
60yds (55m) of super-bulky (chunky) yarn
1 set of 5 dpns size 15 (10mm)
2 sets of size 15 (10mm) circular needles

NOTIONS

Blunt-ended tapestry needle
Toy filling
Row counter

GAUGE (TENSION)

SMALL 30 sts x 39 rows to 4in (10cm) over st st
MEDIUM 18 sts x 25 rows to 4in (10cm) over st st
LARGE 7.5 sts x 10 rows to 4in (10cm) over st st

FINISHED SIZE (APPROX)

SMALL 5¼in x 4in (13.5cm x 10cm)
MEDIUM 9in x 6¾in (23cm x 17cm)
LARGE 15¾in x 13¾in (40cm x 35cm)

YARN CHOICES

Small: Patons Diploma Gold 4ply Iced Green 04198

Medium: Rowan Pure Wool Aran Banana 698

Large: (not shown) Rowan Big Wool or any similar weight super-bulky (chunky) yarn

GET KNITTING

Beginning at bottom of letter with RS facing, work as folls:

Using simple sock cast on method (see Techniques), cast on 38 sts, (19 sts on each ndl).

Rnd 1 (inc) K1, kfb, k15, kfb, k1, k1, kfb, k15, kfb, k1. (42 sts)

Divide sts equally between 2 circular ndls (21 sts on each ndl), with yarn at tip of RH ndl – have LH sts at top of ndl to be worked. PM.

Rnd 2 K42.

Rnd 3 (inc) K1, kfb, k17, kfb, k1, k1, kfb, k17, kfb, k1. (46 sts)

Rnd 4 K46.

Rnd 5 (inc) K1, kfb, k19, kfb, k1, k1, kfb, k19, kfb, k1. (50 sts)

Rnd 6 K50.

Rnd 7 (inc) K1, kfb, k21, kfb, k1, k1, kfb, k21, kfb, k1. (54 sts)

Rnd 8 K54.

Divide for left side

Rnd 9 K1, kfb, k6, k2tog, bind (cast) off 8 sts, k6, kfb, k1, k1, kfb, k6, k2tog, bind (cast) off 8 sts, k6, kfb, k1.

Right side

Rnd 10 K10, sl next 10 sts off circular ndl onto a dpn and set aside, sl next 10 sts off circular ndl and onto another dpn and set aside, k10 for back of right side, working on these 20 sts only join in rnd and cont as folls:

Rnd 11 (inc) K1, kfb, k8, k8, kfb, k1. (22 sts)

Rnds 12 & 13 K22.

Rnd 14 K1, kfb, k6, k2tog, k1, k1, skpo, k6, kfb, k1.

Rnds 15 & 16 K22.

Rnd 17 (dec) K1, skpo, k5, k2tog, k1, k1, skpo, k5, k2tog, k1. (18 sts)

Rnd 18 K18.

Rnd 19 (dec) K1, skpo, k3, k2tog, k1, k1, skpo, k3, k2tog, k1. (14 sts)

Rnd 20 K14.

Rnd 21 (dec) K1, skpo, k1, k2tog, k1, k1, skpo, k1, k2tog, k1. (10 sts)

Cut yarn leaving a tail end 6 times the length of sts on one needle.

Hold 2 sets of 5 sts parallel in your left hand. Thread cut yarn end with a sewing needle then work Kitchener stitch (see Techniques) to close the seam neatly. Weave in tail end.

Left side

With RS facing and with dpns (or spare circulars) rejoin yarn to inner edge and cont as folls:

Rnd 10 (inc) K8, kfb, k1, k1, kfb, k8. (22 sts)

Join in the rnd.

Rnds 11 & 12 K22.

Rnds 13 K1, skpo, k6, kfb, k1, k1, kfb, k6, k2tog, k1.

Rnds 14 & 15 K22.

Rnd 16 (inc) K9, kfb, k1, k1, kfb, k9. (24 sts)

Rnd 17 K24.

Rnd 18 K1, skpo, k7, kfb, k1, k1, kfb, k7, k2tog, k1.

Rnd 19 K24.

Rep last rnd 22 times.

Rnd 42 K1, skpo, k7, kfb, k1, k1, kfb, k7, k2tog, k1.

Rnd 43 K24.

Rnd 44 (dec) K9, k2tog, k1, k1, skpo, k9. (22 sts)

Rnds 45 & 46 K22.

Rnd 47 K1, skpo, k6, kfb, k1, k1, kfb, k6, k2tog, k1.

Rnds 48 & 49 K22.

Rnd 50 (dec) K8, k2tog, k1, k1, skpo, k8. (20 sts)

Rnd 51 (inc) Cast on 15 sts, k35, WS (purl side) of work facing, cast on 15 sts, join into a rnd without twisting sts. (50 sts)

Shape serif

Work short rows (see Techniques) as folls:

Short row 1 K5, w+t.

Short row 2 P10, w+t.

Short row 3 K9, w+t.

Short row 4 P8, w+t.

Short row 5 K7, w+t.

Short row 6 P6, w+t.

Short row 7 K5, w+t.

Short row 8 P4, w+t.

Short row 9 K3, w+t.

Short row 10 P2, w+t.

Short row 11 K1.

Rnd 52 (dec) K1, skpo, k19, k2tog, k1, k1, skpo, k19, k2tog, k1. (46 sts)

Rnd 53 K46.

Rnd 54 (dec) K1, skpo, k17, k2tog, k1, k1, skpo, k17, k2tog, k1. (42 sts)

Rnd 55 K42.

Rnd 56 (dec) K1, skpo, k15, k2tog, k1, k1, skpo, k15, k2tog, k1. (38 sts)

Rnd 57 K38.

Rep last rnd 3 times.

Cut yarn leaving a tail end 5 times the length of sts on one needle.

TO FINISH OFF

Hold 2 sets of 19 sts parallel in your left hand. Thread cut yarn end with a sewing needle then work Kitchener stitch to close the seam neatly.

Stuff the letter firmly and evenly through the openings. Close the opening with mattress stitch. Weave in tail ends.

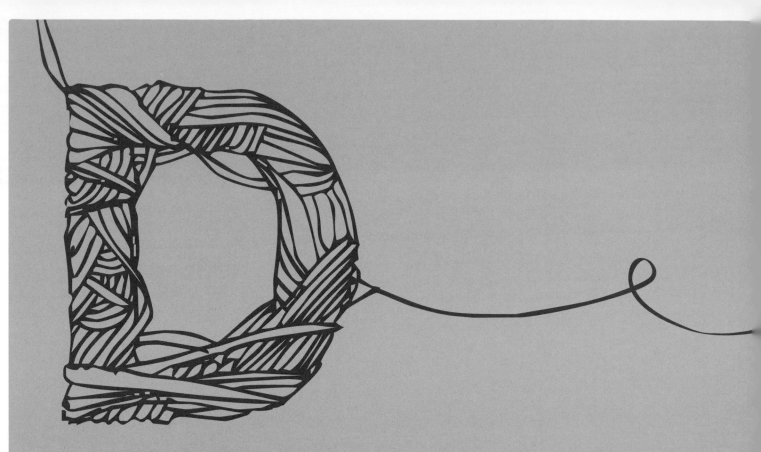

YOU WILL NEED

SMALL
37yds (34m) of fingering-weight (4ply) yarn
1 set of dpns size 1 (2.5mm)
2 sets of size 1 (2.5mm) circular needles

MEDIUM
104yds (95m) of worsted weight (Aran) yarn
1 set of 5 dpns size 8 (5mm)
2 sets of size 8 (5mm) circular needles

LARGE
118yds (108m) of bulky weight (chunky) yarn
1 set of 5 dpns size 15 (10mm)
2 sets of size 15 (10mm) circular needles

NOTIONS
Blunt-ended tapestry needle
Toy filling
Row counter
2 spare dpns for stitch holders

GAUGE (TENSION)

SMALL 30 sts x 39 rows to 4in (10cm) over st st
MEDIUM 18 sts x 25 rows to 4in (10cm) over st st
LARGE 7.5 sts x 10 rows to 4in (10cm) over st st

FINISHED SIZE (APPROX)

SMALL 5¼in x 3½in (13.5cm x 9cm)
MEDIUM 9½in x 9in (24cm x 23cm)
LARGE 15¾in x 13¾in (40cm x 35cm)

YARN CHOICES

Small: Patons Fairytale Dreamtime
4ply Hot Pink 02939
Medium: Rowan Pure Wool Aran Ivory 670
Large: Rowan Big Wool Ice Blue 021

GET KNITTING

Beginning at the bottom of letter with RS facing work as folls:

Using simple sock cast on method (see Techniques), cast on 52 sts, (26 sts on each ndl).

Rnd 1 K52.

Divide sts equally between 2 circular ndls (26 sts on each ndl), with yarn at tip of RH ndl – have LH sts at top of ndl to be worked. PM.

Rnd 2 (inc) K1, kfb, k24, k24, kfb, k1. (54 sts)

Rnd 3 (dec) Kfb, k21, skpo, k2tog, k1, k1, skpo, k2tog, k21, kfb. (52 sts)

Rnd 4 (inc) K1, kfb, k24, k24, kfb, k1. (54 sts)

Rnd 5 (dec) Kfb, k21, skpo, k2tog, k1, k1, skpo, k2tog, k21, kfb. (52 sts)

Rep last 2 rnds once.

Rnd 8 (inc) K1, kfb, k24, k24, kfb, k1. (54 sts)

Divide straight side from curved side

Rnd 9 K1, kfb, k6, k2tog, bind (cast) off 6 sts, k10, k11 bind (cast) off 7 sts, k6, kfb, k1.

Curved side

Rnd 10 K10, sl next 11 sts off circular ndl and onto a dpn and set aside, sl next 11 sts off circular ndl and onto another dpn and set aside, k10 for back of right side, working on these 20 sts only join in rnd and cont as folls:

Rnd 11 (inc) K1, kfb, k8, k8, kfb, k1. (22 sts)

Rnds 12 & 13 K22.

Rnd 14 K1, kfb, k6, k2tog, k1, k1, skpo, k6, kfb, k1.

Rnds 15 &16 K22.

Rnd 17 K1, kfb, k9, k9, kfb, k1. (24 sts)

Rnd 18 K24.

Rnd 19 K1, kfb, k7, k2tog, k1, k1, skpo, k7, kfb, k1.

Rnds 20–41 K24.

Rnd 42 K1, skpo, k7, kfb, k1, k1, kfb, k7, k2tog, k1.

Rnd 43 K24.

Rnd 44 (dec) K1, skpo, k9, k9, k2tog, k1. (22 sts).

Rnds 45 & 46 K22.

Rnd 47 K1, skpo, k6, kfb, k1, k1, kfb, k6, k2tog, k1.

Rnds 48 & 49 K22.

Rnd 50 (dec) K1, skpo, k8, k8, k2tog, k1. (20 sts)

Rnd 51 K20.

Set these sts aside and return to sts on dpns to work straight side.

Left side

With RS facing and dpns (or spare circulars) join other end of yarn (or new ball) to inner edge and cont as folls:

Rnd 9 K22.

Rep last rnd 42 times. Cut yarn.

Join curved side with straight side

With RS facing cont as folls:

Rnd 52 (inc) K1, skpo, k5, kfb, k1, backward loop cast on 4 sts, k across first set of 11 sts from straight side – (25 sts on ndl), sl 2nd set of 11 sts from straight side onto second circular ndl then k across, backward loop cast on 4 sts, then work across rem sts from curved side as folls: k1, kfb, k5, k2tog, k1 (25 sts on second circular ndl). Join in the rnd.

Rnd 53 (inc) K23, kfb, k1, k1, kfb, k23. (52 sts)

Rnd 54 (inc) Skpo, k22, m1, k1, kfb, kfb, k1, m1, k22, k2tog. (54 sts)

Rnd 55 (dec) K1, skpo, k24, k24, k2tog, k1. (52 sts)

Rnd 56 (inc) Skpo, k22, m1, k1, kfb, kfb, k1, m1, k22, k2tog, k1. (54 sts)

Rnd 57 K1, skpo, k24, k24, k2tog, k1. (52 sts)

Rnd 58 Skpo, k22, m1, k1, kfb, kfb, k1, m1, k22, k2tog. (54 sts)

Rnd 59 K1, skpo, k24, k24, k2tog, k1. (52 sts)

Cut yarn leaving a tail end 6 times the length of the sts on one ndl.

TO FINISH OFF

Hold 2 sets of 26 sts parallel in your left hand. Thread cut yarn end with a sewing needle then work Kitchener stitch (see Techniques) to close the seam neatly.

Stuff the letter firmly and evenly through the opening. Close the opening with mattress stitch. Weave in tail ends.

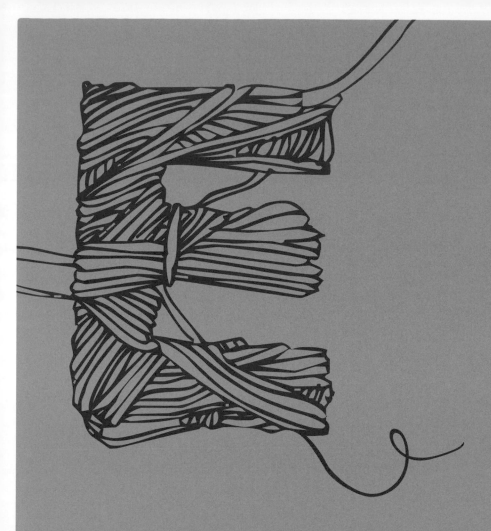

YOU WILL NEED

SMALL
55yds (50m) of fingering-weight (4ply) yarn
1 set of 5dpns size 1 (2.5mm)
2 sets of size 1 (2.5mm) circular needles

MEDIUM
75yds (68m) of worsted weight (Aran) yarn
1 set of 5 dpns size 8 (5mm)
2 sets of size 8 (5mm) circular needles

LARGE
118yds (108m) of super bulky (chunky) yarn
1 set of 5 dpns size 15 (10mm)
2 sets of size 15 (10mm) circular needles

NOTIONS
Blunt-ended tapestry needle
Toy filling
Row counter
2 spare dpns for stitch holders

GAUGE (TENSION)

SMALL 30 sts x 39 rows to 4in (10cm) over st st

MEDIUM 18 sts x 25 rows to 4in (10cm) over st st

LARGE 7.5 sts x 10 rows to 4in (10cm) over st st

FINISHED SIZE (APPROX)

SMALL 5¼in x 4¼in (13.5cm x 11cm)

MEDIUM 9in x 6¼in (23cm x 16cm)

LARGE 15¾in x 13¾in (40cm x 35cm)

GET KNITTING

Beginning at the bottom of letter working with RS facing work as folls:

Using simple sock cast on method (see Techniques), cast on 60 sts, (30 sts on each ndl).

Rnd 1 K60.

Divide sts equally between 2 circular ndls (30 sts on each ndl), with yarn at tip of RH ndl – have LH sts at top of ndl to be worked. PM.

Rnds 2 & 3 K60.

Rnd 4 (inc) K1, kfb, k28, k28, kfb, k1. (62 sts)

Rnd 5 (inc) Kfb, k30, k30, kfb. (64 sts)

Rnd 6 (dec) K1, kfb, k26, skpo, k2tog, skpo, k2tog, k26, kfb, k1. (62 sts)

Rnd 7 (inc) K1, kfb, k29, k29, kfb, k1. (64 sts)

Shape serif

Work short rows (see Techniques) as folls:

Short Row 1 K6, w&t.

Short Row 2 P12, w&t.

Short Row 3 K11, w&t.

Short Row 4 P10, w&t.

Short Row 5 K9, w&t.

Short Row 6 P8, w&t.

Short Row 7 K7, w&t.

Short Row 8 P6, w&t.

Short Row 9 K5, w&t.

Short Row 10 P4, w&t.

Short Row 11 K3, w&t.

Short Row 12 P2, w&t.

Short Row 13 K1.

Cut yarn leaving a tail twice the length of sts on one ndl.

Using Kitchener stitch, (see Techniques), graft together the next 2 sets of 21 sts (21 sts from each ndl thus 42 sts in total). 11 sts rem on each ndl (22 sts total).

Lower left straight edge

With RS facing rejoin yarn to rem sts and join into a rnd.

Rnd 8 K22.

Rep last rnd 17 times.

Middle bar

Rnd 26 (inc) Cast on 12 sts, k34, with WS facing, cast on 12 sts, without twisting sts join in the rnd. (48 sts)

Middle bar lower serif

Work short rows as folls:

Short row 1 *K5, w+t.

Short row 2 P10, w+t.

Short row 3 K9, w+t.

Short row 4 P8, w+t.

Short row 5 K7, w+t.

Short row 6 P6, w+t.

Short row 7 K5, w+t.

Short row 8 P4, w+t.

Short row 9 K3, w+t.

Short row 10 P2, w+t.

Short row 11 K1*.

Cont to work in rnds as folls:

Rnd 27 K46.

Rep last rnd 5 times.

Middle bar upper serif

Work as for middle bar lower serif from * to *.

Cut yarn leaving a tail twice the length of sts on one ndl.

Using Kitchener stitch, graft together the next 2 sets of 12 sts (12 sts from each ndl thus 24 sts in total). 11 sts rem on each ndl.

Upper left straight edge

With RS of letter facing, rejoin yarn to rem 22 sts.

Rnd 33 K22. Join in the rnd.

Rep last rnd 17 times.

Upper bar

Rnd 51 (inc) Cast on 15 sts, k37, with WS facing cast on 15 sts, without twisting sts join in the rnd. (52 sts)

Shape serif

Work as for middle bar lower serif from * to *.

Rnd 52 K52.

Rnd 53 (inc) K24, m1, k1, kfb, kfb, k1, m1, k24. (56 sts)

Rnd 54 K56.

Rnd 55 (inc) K26, m1, k1, kfb, kfb, k1, m1, k26. (60 sts)

Rnd 56 K60.

Rep last rnd 4 times.

Cut yarn leaving a tail end 6 times the length of sts on one ndl.

TO FINISH OFF

Stuff letter firmly and evenly. Hold two sets of 30 sts parallel in your left hand. Thread cut yarn end with a sewing ndl then work Kitchener stitch to close the seam neatly. Weave in tail end.

YOU WILL NEED

SMALL
35yds (32m) of fingering-weight (4ply) yarn
1 set of 5 dpns size 1 (2.5mm)
2 sets of size 1 (2.5mm) circular needles

MEDIUM
47yds (43m) of worsted weight (Aran) yarn
1 set of 5 dpns size 8 (5mm)
2 set of size 8 (5mm) circular needles

LARGE
110yds (100m) of bulky weight (chunky) yarn
1 set of 5 dpns size 15 (10mm)
2 sets of size 15 (10mm) circular needles

NOTIONS
Blunt-ended tapestry needle
Toy filling
Row counter

GAUGE (TENSION)
SMALL 30 sts x 39 rows to 4in (10cm) over st st
MEDIUM 18 sts x 22 rows to 4in (10cm) over st st
LARGE 7.5 sts x 10 rows to 4in (10cm) over st st

FINISHED SIZE (APPROX)
SMALL 4in x 2¼in (10.5cm x 6.5cm)
MEDIUM 6in x 5in (15cm x 13cm)
LARGE 15¾in x 13¾in (40cm x 35cm)

YARN CHOICES

Small: Rowan Pure Wool 4ply Framboise 456

Medium: (not shown) Rowan Pure Wool Aran Vert 686 and small amount Splash 701

Large: Rowan Big Wool Lipstick 063, Heather 058, Linen 048

GET KNITTING

Beginning at the bottom of letter working with RS facing work as folls:

Using simple sock cast on method (see Techniques), cast on 38 sts, (19 sts on each ndl).

Rnd 1 K38.

Divide sts equally between 2 circular ndls (19 sts on each ndl), with yarn at tip of RH ndl – have LH sts at top of ndl to be worked. PM.

Rnds 2–4 K38.

Rnd 5 (dec) Skpo, k2tog, k11, skpo, k2tog, skpo, k2tog, k11, skpo, k2tog. (30 sts)

Rnd 6 K30.

Rnd 7 (dec) Skpo, k2tog, k7, skpo, k2tog, skpo, k2tog, k7, skpo, k2tog. (22 sts)

Rnd 8 K22.

Rep last rnd 17 times.

Middle bar

Rnd 26 Cast on 12 sts, k34, WS of knitting facing, cast on 12 sts, without twisting sts join in the rnd. (46 sts)

Shape lower serif

Work short rows (see Techniques) as folls:

Short row 1 *K5, w+t.

Short row 2 P10, w+t.

Short row 3 K9, w+t.

Short row 4 P8, w+t.

Short row 5 K7, w+t.

Short row 6 P6, w+t.

Short row 7 K5, w+t.

Short row 8 P4, w+t.

Short row 9 K3, w+t.

Short row 10 P2, w+t.

Short row 11 K1*.

Cont to work in rnds as folls:

Rnd 27 K46.

Rep last rnd 5 times.

Shape upper serif

Work short rows as for lower serif from * to *.

Cut yarn leaving a tail twice the length of sts on one ndl.

Using Kitchener stitch, graft together next 2 sets of 12 sts (12 sts from each ndl thus 24 sts in total). 11 sts rem on each ndl.

Upper left straight edge

With RS of letter facing, rejoin yarn to rem 22 sts.

Rnd 33 K22.

Rep last rnd 17 times.

Upper bar

Rnd 51 (inc) Cast on 15 sts, k37, with WS facing cast on 15 sts, without twisting sts join in the rnd. (52 sts)

Shape serif

Work as for lower serif from * to *.

Rnd 52 K52.

Rnd 53 (inc) K24, m1, k1, kfb, kfb, k1, m1, k24. (56 sts)

Rnd 54 K56.

Rnd 55 (inc) K26, m1, k1, kfb, kfb, k1, m1, k26. (60 sts)

Rnd 56 K60.

Rep last rnd 4 times.

Cut yarn leaving a tail end 6 times the length of sts on one ndl.

TO FINISH OFF

Stuff letter firmly and evenly. Hold two sets of 30 sts parallel in your left hand. Thread cut yarn end with a sewing ndl then work Kitchener stitch to close the seam neatly. Weave in tail end.

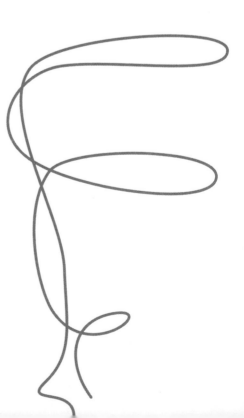

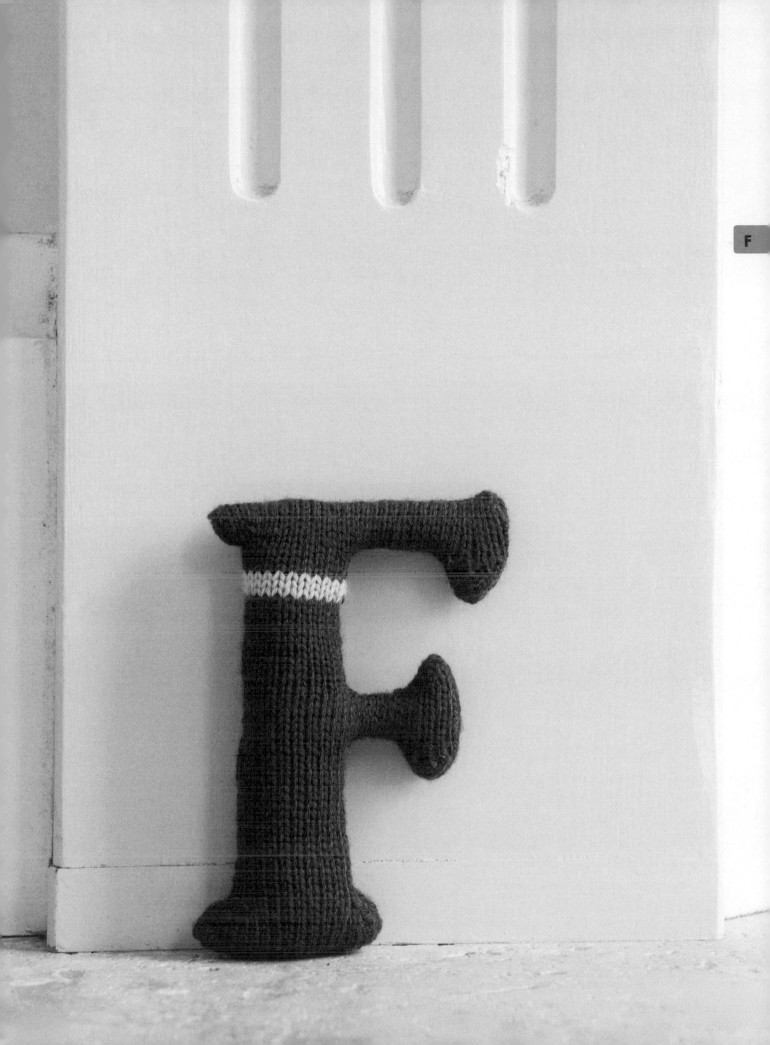

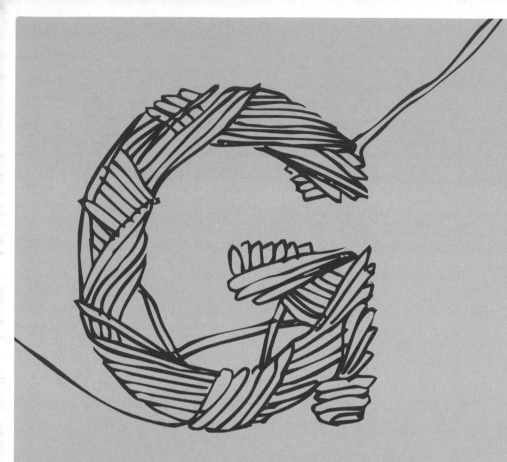

YOU WILL NEED

SMALL
22yds (20m) of fingering-weight (4ply) yarn
1 set of 5 dpns size 8 (5mm)
2 sets of size 8 (5mm) circular needles

MEDIUM
80yds (73m) of worsted weight (Aran) yarn
1 set of 5 dpns size 8 (5mm)
2 set of size 8 (5mm) circular needles

LARGE
109yds (100m) of super-bulky (chunky) yarn
1 set of 5 dpns size 15 (10mm)
2 sets of size 15 (10mm) circular needles

NOTIONS
Blunt-ended tapestry needle
2 spare dpns for stitch holders
Toy filling
Row counter

GAUGE (TENSION)
SMALL 30 sts x 39 rows to 4in (10cm) over st st
MEDIUM 18 sts x 25 rows to 4in (10cm) over st st
LARGE 7.5 sts x 10 rows to 4in (10cm) over st st

FINISHED SIZE (APPROX)
SMALL 5¼in x 4in (13.5cm x 10cm)
MEDIUM 9in x 6¾in (23cm x 17cm)
LARGE 15¾in x 13¼in (40cm x 34cm)

Beginning at the bottom of letter working with RS facing work as folls:

Using simple sock cast on method (see Techniques), cast on 38 sts, (19 sts on each ndl).

Rnd 1 (inc) K1, kfb, k15, kfb, k1, k1, kfb, k15, kfb, k1. (42 sts)

Divide sts equally between 2 circular ndls (21 sts on each ndl), with yarn at tip of RH ndl – have LH sts at top of ndl to be worked. PM.

Rnd 2 K42.

Rnd 3 (inc) K1, kfb, k17, kfb, k1, k1, kfb, k17, kfb, k1. (46 sts)

Rnd 4 K46.

Rnd 5 (inc) K1, kfb, k19, kfb, k1, k1, kfb, k19, kfb, k1. (50 sts)

Rnd 6 K50.

Rnd 7 (inc) K1, kfb, k21, kfb, k1, k1, kfb, k21, kfb, k1. (54 sts)

Rnd 8 K54.

Divide for left side

Rnd 9 K1, kfb, k6, k2tog, bind (cast) off 8 sts, k6, kfb, k1, k1, kfb, k6, k2tog, bind (cast) off 8 sts, k6, kfb, k1.

Right side

Rnd 10 K10, sl next 10 sts off circular ndl and onto a dpn and set aside, sl next 10 sts off circular ndl and onto another dpn and set aside, k10 for back of right side, working on these 20 sts only join in rnd and cont as folls:

Rnd 11 (inc) K1, kfb, k8, k8, kfb, k1. (22 sts)

Rnds 12 & 13 K22.

Rnd 14 K1, kfb, k6, k2tog, k1, k1, skpo, k6, kfb, k1.

Rnd 15 K22.

Rep last rnd 7 times.

Rnd 23 (inc) Kfb, k1, m1, k7, m1, k1, kfb, kfb, k1, m1, k7, m1, k1, kfb. (30 sts)

Rnd 24 K30.

Rnd 25 (inc) Kfb, k1, m1, k11, m1, k1, kfb, kfb, k1, m1, k11, m1, k1, kfb. (38 sts)

Rnd 26 K38.

Rep last rnd 3 times.

Cut yarn leaving a tail end 6 times the length of the sts on one needle.

Hold 2 sets of 10 sts parallel in your left hand. Thread cut yarn end with a sewing needle then work Kitchener stitch (see Techniques) to close the seam neatly. Weave in tail end.

Left side

With RS facing and with dpns (or spare circulars) rejoin yarn to inner edge and cont as folls:

Rnd 10 (inc) K8, kfb, k1, k1, kfb, k8. (22 sts)

Rnds 11 & 12 K22.

Rnds 13 K1, skpo, k6, kfb, k1, k1, kfb, k6, k2tog, k1.

Rnds 14 & 15 K22.

Rnd 16 (inc) K9, kfb, k1, k1, kfb, k9. (24 sts)

Rnd 17 K24.

Rnd 18 K1, skpo, k7, kfb, k1, k1, kfb, k7, k2tog, k1.

Rnd 19 K24.

Rep last rnd 22 times.

Rnd 42 K1, skpo, k7, kfb, k1, k1, kfb, k7, k2tog, k1.

Rnd 43 K24.

Rnd 44 (dec) K9, k2tog, k1, k1, skpo, k9. (22 sts)

Rnds 45 & 46 K22.

Rnd 47 K1, skpo, k6, kfb, k1, k1, kfb, k6, k2tog, k1.

Rnds 48 & 49 K22.

Rnd 50 (dec) K8, k2tog, k1, k1, skpo, k8. (20 sts)

Rnd 51 (inc) Cast on 15 sts, k35, WS (purl side) of work facing, cast on 15 sts, join into a rnd without twisting sts. (50 sts)

Shape serif

Work short rows (see Techniques) as folls:

Short row 1 K5, w+t.

Short row 2 P10, w+t.

Short row 3 K9, w+t.

Short row 4 P8, w+t.

Short row 5 K7, w+t.

Short row 6 P6, w+t.

Short row 7 K5, w+t.

Short row 8 P4, w+t.

Short row 9 K3, w+t.

Short row 10 P2, w+t.

Short row 11 K1.

Rnd 52 (dec) K1, skpo, k19, k2tog, k1, k1, skpo, k19, k2tog, k1. (46 sts)

Rnd 53 K46.

Rnd 54 (dec) K1, skpo, k17, k2tog, k1, k1, skpo, k17, k2tog, k1. (42 sts)

Rnd 55 K42.

Rnd 56 (dec) K1, skpo, k15, k2tog, k1, k1, skpo, k15, k2tog, k1. (38 sts)

Rnd 57 K38.

Rep last rnd 3 times.

Cut yarn leaving a tail end 5 times the length of sts on one needle.

TO FINISH OFF

Hold 2 sets of 19 sts parallel in your left hand. Thread cut yarn end with a sewing needle then work Kitchener stitch to close the seam neatly

Stuff the letter firmly and evenly through the openings. Close the opening with mattress stitch. Weave in tail ends.

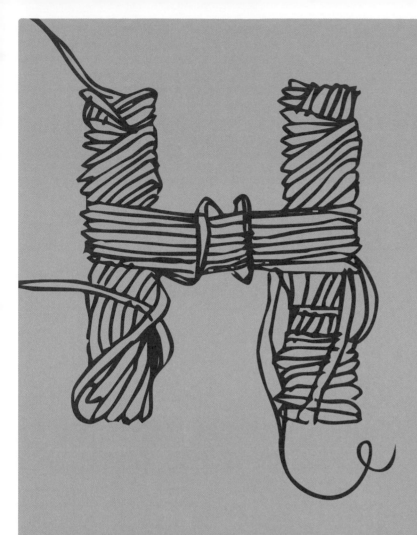

YOU WILL NEED

SMALL
52½yds (48m) of fingering-weight (4ply) yarn
1 set of 5 dpns size 1 (2.5mm)
2 sets of size 1 (2.5mm) circular needles

MEDIUM
91yds (83m) of worsted weight (Aran) yarn
1 set of 5 dpns size 8 (5mm)
2 sets of size 8 (5mm) circular needles

LARGE
112yds (102m) of super-bulky (chunky) yarn
1 set of 5 dpns size 15 (10mm)
2 sets of size 15 (10mm) circular needles

NOTIONS
Blunt-ended tapestry needle
2 spare dpns as stitch holders
Toy filling
Row counter

GAUGE (TENSION)
SMALL 30 sts x 39 rows to 4in (10cm) over st st
MEDIUM 18 sts x 25 rows to 4in (10cm) over st st
LARGE 7.5 sts x 10 rows to 4in (10cm) over st st

FINISHED SIZE (APPROX)
SMALL 5¼in x 4¾in (13.5cm x 12cm)
MEDIUM 9in x 8¾in (23cm x 22cm)
LARGE 15¾in x 13¾in (40cm x 35cm)

YARN CHOICES

Small: Rowan Pure Wool 4ply Eau de Nil 450 and Rowan Cashsoft 4ply Elite 451

Medium: Rowan Pure Wool Aran Indigo 694

Large: (not shown) Rowan Big Wool or any similar weight super-bulky (chunky) yarn

Left leg

Beginning at bottom of leg with RS facing, work as folls:

Using simple sock cast on method (see Techniques), cast on 38 sts, (19 sts on each ndl).

Rnd 1 K38.

Divide sts equally between 2 circular ndls (19 sts on each ndl), with yarn at tip of RH ndl – have LH sts at top of ndl to be worked. PM.

Rnds 2–4 K38.

Rnd 5 (dec) Skpo, k2tog, k11, skpo, k2tog, skpo, k2tog, k11, skpo, k2tog. (30 sts)

Rnd 6 K30.

Rnd 7 (dec) Skpo, k2tog, k7, skpo, k2tog, skpo, k2tog, k7, skpo, k2tog. (22 sts)

Rnd 8 K22.

Rep last rnd 17 times.**

Cut yarn and sl 2 sets of sts onto dpns and set aside.

Right leg

Cast on 38 sts and work as for left leg to **.

Join legs together with central bar

Rnd 26 K11 from front of right side, onto same ndl backward loop cast on 12 sts, k11 sts held on dpn from front of left side. Slide rem 11 sts from dpn onto second circular ndl – (back sts of right side will be facing you), k these 11 sts, backward loop cast on 12 sts, k11 from back right side. (68 sts, 34 sts on each ndl)

Rnd 27 Knit.

Rep last rnd 7 times.

Rnd 35 K23, slide last 12 sts from central bar onto a dpn, onto another dpn k next 11 sts from left front. Onto a third dpn k next 23 sts, slide last 12 sts from central bar onto a fourth dpn. K rem 11 sts from right back onto circular ndl. (Thus both sets of right leg sts are on circulars, the two sets of central bar sts are held on dpns ready for grafting. The two sets 11 left leg sts are held on dpns to be worked on later.)

Graft central bar

Using yarn from other end of ball band cut a length that measures 3 times the length of sts on one side of the letter.

Hold two sets of 12 sts parallel in your left hand. Using a yarn sewing needle secure the length of cut yarn before starting to knit at the end to the right of the front set of 12 sts, then work Kitchener stitch (see Techniques) to close seam neatly. Weave in tail end.

Complete right side

Cont with right side sts as folls:

Rnd 36 K22.

*Rep last rnd 17 times.

Rnd 54 (inc) Kfb, k1, m1, k7, m1, k1, kfb, kfb, k1, m1, k7, m1, k1, kfb. (30 sts)

Rnd 55 K30.

Rnd 56 (inc) Kfb, k1, m1, k11, m1, k1, kfb, kfb, k1, m1, k11, m1, k1, kfb. (38 sts)

Rnd 57 K38.

Rep last rnd 3 times.

Cut yarn leaving a tail end 6 times the length of sts on one ndl.

Hold two sets of 19 sts parallel in your left hand. Thread cut yarn end with a sewing ndl then work Kitchener st to close seam neatly. Weave in tail end.**

Complete left side

With RS facing rejoin yarn to 11 sts at front of left side – working with dpns or circulars, cont as folls:

Rnd 36 K11 sts across front and 11 sts across back of left side. (22 sts)

Join in the rnd.

Cont as right side from * to **.

TO FINISH OFF

Stuff letter firmly and evenly through opening. Close opening with mattress stitch.

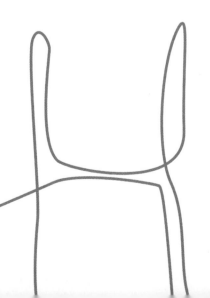

YOU WILL NEED

SMALL

16½yds (15m) of fingering-weight (4ply) yarn
1 set of 5 dpns size 1 (2.5mm)
2 sets of size 1 (2.5mm) circular needles

MEDIUM

43yds (39m) of worsted weight (Aran) yarn
1 set of 5 dpns size 8 (5mm)
2 sets of size 8 (5mm) circular needles

LARGE

60yds (55m) of super-bulky (chunky) yarn
1 set of 5 dpns size 15 (10mm)
2 sets of 15 (10mm) circular needles

NOTIONS

Blunt-ended tapestry needle
Toy filling
Row counter

GAUGE (TENSION)

SMALL 30 sts x 39 rows to 4in (10cm) over st st
MEDIUM 18 sts x 25 rows to 4in (10cm) over st st
LARGE 7.5 sts x 10 rows to 4in (10cm) over st st

FINISHED SIZE (APPROX)

SMALL 5¼in x 2¼in (13.5cm x 5.5cm)
MEDIUM 8¾in x 4in (22cm x 10cm)
LARGE 15¾in x 7in (38cm x 18cm)

YARN CHOICES

Small: Rowan Pure Wool 4ply Eau de Nil 450, Framboise 456

Medium: Rowan Pure Wool Aran Ivory 670, Burnt 700

Large: (not shown) Rowan Big Wool or any similar weight super-bulky (chunky) yarn

GET KNITTING

Beginning at the bottom of letter working with RS facing work as folls:

Using simple sock cast on method (see Techniques), cast on 38 sts, (19 sts on each ndl).

Rnd 1 K38.

Divide sts equally between 2 circular ndls (19 sts on each ndl), with yarn at tip of RH ndl – have LH sts at top of ndl to be worked. PM.

Rnds 2–4 K38.

Rnd 5 (dec) Skpo, k2tog, k11, skpo, k2tog, skpo, k2tog, k11, skpo, k2tog. (30 sts)

Rnd 6 K30.

Rnd 7 (dec) Skpo, k2tog, k7, skpo, k2tog, skpo, k2tog, k7, skpo, k2tog. (22 sts)

Rnd 8 K22.

Rep last rnd 45 times.

Rnd 54 (inc) Kfb, k1, m1, k7, m1, k1, kfb, kfb, k1, m1, k7, m1, k1, kfb. (30 sts)

Rnd 55 K30.

Rnd 56 (inc) Kfb, k1, m1, k11, m1, k1, kfb, kfb, k1, m1, k11, m1, k1, kfb. (38 sts)

Rnd 57 K38.

Rep last rnd 3 times.

Cut yarn leaving a tail end 6 times the length of sts on one ndl.

TO FINISH OFF

Stuff letter firmly and evenly.

Hold two sets of 19 sts parallel in your left hand. Thread cut yarn end with a sewing ndl then work Kitchener stitch to close the seam neatly. Weave in tail end.

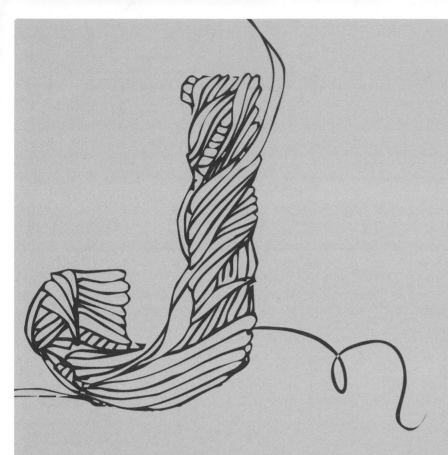

YOU WILL NEED

SMALL
18½yds (17m) of fingering-weight (4ply) yarn
1 set of 5 dpns size 1 (2.5mm)
2 sets of size 1 (2.5mm) circular needles

MEDIUM
47yds (43m) of worsted weight (Aran) yarn
1 set of 5 dpns size 8 (5mm)
2 sets of size 8 (5mm) circular needles

LARGE
80yds (73m) of super-bulky (chunky) yarn
1 set of 5 dpns size 15 (10mm)
2 sets of size 15 (10mm) circular needles

NOTIONS
Blunt-ended tapestry needle
Toy filling
Row counter

GAUGE (TENSION)
SMALL 30 sts x 39 rows to 4in (10cm) over st st
MEDIUM 18 sts x 25 rows to 4in (10cm) over st st
LARGE 7.5 sts x 10 rows to 4in (10cm) over st st

FINISHED SIZE (APPROX)
SMALL 5½in x 3¼in (14cm x 8cm)
MEDIUM 9in x 6in (23cm x 15.5cm)
LARGE 16½in x 13¾in (42cm x 35cm)

J

GET KNITTING

Beginning at the bottom of letter working with RS facing work curved tip as folls:

Using simple sock cast on method (see Techniques), cast on 6 sts, (3 sts on each ndl).

Rnd 1 Kfb 6 times. (12 sts)

Rnd 2 (inc) Kfb, k4, kfb, kfb, k4, kfb. (16 sts)

Divide sts equally between 2 circular ndls (8 sts on each ndl), with yarn at tip of RH ndl – have LH sts at top of ndl to be worked. PM.

Rnd 3 inc K1, kfb, k4, kfb, k1, k1, kfb, k4, kfb, k1. (20 sts)

Rnd 4 K20.

Rep last rnd once.

Rnd 6 (inc) Kfb, k8, kfb, kfb, k8, kfb. (24 sts)

Rnd 7 K24.

Rnd 8 (dec) K1, skpo, k6, k2tog, k1, k1, skpo, k6, k2tog, k1. (20 sts)

Rnd 9 K20.

Rnd 10 (dec) K1, skpo, k4, k2tog, k1, k1, skpo, k4, k2tog, k1. (16 sts)

Rnd 11 K16.

Rnd 12 (dec) (side A) K1, skpo, k5, (side B) k5, k2tog, k1. (14 sts)

Cut yarn, slip 2 sets sts onto two dpns.

Straight side

With side A facing cont as folls:

Cast on 38 sts onto one ndl then using simple sock cast on.

Rnd 1 K38.

Divide sts equally between 2 circular ndls (19 sts on each ndl), with yarn at tip of RH ndl – have LH sts at top of ndl to be worked. PM.

Rnds 2–4 K38.

Rnd 5 (dec) Skpo, k2tog, k11, skpo, k2tog, skpo, k2tog, k11, skpo, k2tog. (30 sts)

Rnd 6 K30.

Rnd 7 (dec) Skpo, k2tog, k7, skpo, k2tog, skpo, k2tog, k7, skpo, k2tog. (22 sts)

Rnd 8 K22.

Rep last rnd 36 times.

Shape curve

Rnd 45 K1, skpo, k6, kfb, k1, k1, kfb, k6, k2tog, k1.

Rnd 46 K22.

Rep last 2 rnds twice.

Rnd 51 (dec) K1, skpo, k2tog, k5, kfb, kfb, k5, skpo, k2tog, k1. (20 sts)

Rnd 52 K20.

Rnd 53 (dec) K1, skpo, k2tog, k4, kfb, kfb, k4, skpo, k2tog, k1. (18 sts)

Rnd 54 K18.

Join two parts

Rnd 55 (inc) K1, skpo, k6, backward loop cast on 3 sts, then from side A of curved section k4, k2tog, k1 (17 sts on one circular ndl). Turn work, slide other 7 sts from curved section (side B) onto circular ndl with rem sts from straight side, k1, skpo, k4, backward loop cast on 3 sts, k6, k2tog, k1 (17 sts on second circular ndl). (34 sts)

Rnd 56 (dec) K1, skpo, k11, k2tog, k1, k1, skpo, k11, k2tog, k1. (30 sts)

Rnd 57 K30.

Rnd 58 (dec) K1, skpo, k9, k2tog, k1, k1, skpo, k9, k2tog, k1. (26 sts)

Rnd 59 K26.

Rnd 60 (dec) K1, skpo, k7, k2tog, k1, k1, skpo, k7, k2tog, k1. (22 sts)

Rnd 61 K22.

Rnd 62 (dec) K1, skpo, k5, k2tog, k1, k1, skpo, k5, k2tog, k1. (18 sts)

Rnd 63 K18.

TO FINISH OFF

Stuff letter firmly and evenly.

Hold two sets of 9 sts parallel in your left hand. Thread cut yarn end with a sewing ndl then work Kitchener stitch to close the seam neatly. Weave in tail end.

J

YOU WILL NEED

SMALL
35yds (32m) of fingering-weight (4ply) yarn
1 set of 5 dpns size 1 (2.5mm)
2 sets of size 1 (2.5mm) circular needles

MEDIUM
71yds (65m) of worsted weight (Aran) yarn
1 set of 5 dpns size 8 (5mm)
2 sets of size 8 (5mm) circular needles

LARGE
112yds (102m) of super-bulky (chunky) yarn
1 set of 5 dpns size 15 (10mm)
2 sets of size 15 (10mm) circular needles

NOTIONS
Blunt-ended tapestry needle
Toy filling
Row counter

GAUGE (TENSION)
SMALL 30 sts x 39 rows to 4in (10cm) over st st
MEDIUM 18 sts x 25 rows to 4in (10cm) over st st
LARGE 7.5 sts x 10 rows to 4in (10cm) over st st

FINISHED SIZE (APPROX)
SMALL 5in x 4¼in (13cm x 11cm)
MEDIUM 8¼in x 6¾in (21cm x 17cm)
LARGE 15¾in x 13¾in (40cm x 35cm)

K

GET KNITTING

Left side of letter

Beginning at bottom left straight side and with RS facing, using simple sock cast on method (see Techniques), cast on 38 sts.

Rnd 1 K38.

Divide sts equally between 2 circular ndls (19 sts on each ndl), with yarn at tip of RH ndl — have LH sts at top of ndl to be worked. PM.

Rnds 2–4 K38.

Rnd 5 (dec) Skpo, k2tog, k11, skpo, k2tog, skpo, k2tog, k11, skpo, k2tog. (30 sts)

Rnd 6 K30.**

Rnd 7 (dec) Skpo, k2tog, k7, skpo, k2tog, skpo, k2tog, k7, skpo, k2tog. (22 sts)

Rnd 8 K22.

Rep last rnd 15 times.

Cut yarn and sl two sets of sts onto 2 dpns and set aside.

Right (slanting) side of letter

Cast on 38 sts using simple sock method (19 sts on each ndl).

Work as left side of letter to **.

Rnd 7 (dec) Skpo, k2tog, k7, skpo, k2tog, skpo, k2tog, k7, skpo, k2tog. (22 sts)

Rnd 8 K22.

Rnd 9 K1, skpo, k6, kfb, k1, k1, kfb, k6, k2tog, k1.

Rep last 2 rnds 7 times.

Join both sides together

Rnd 24 K11 on circular ndl (ie, from front of right side) onto same ndl backward loop cast on 2 sts, then k11 from front of left side from dpn. Slide rem 11 sts from dpn onto other circular ndl — (back sts of right side should be facing), k these 11 sts, backward loop cast on 2 sts, then k11 from back of right side. (48 sts, 24 sts on each ndl)

Cont to work in rnds pulling tension tight as you knit across joins to avoid gaps and taking care not to twist cast on sts.

Rnd 25 (dec) K1, skpo, k21, k21, k2tog, k1. (46 sts)

Rnd 26 K46.

Rnd 27 (dec) K1, skpo, k20, k20, k2tog, k1. (44 sts)

Rnd 28 K44.

Rnd 29 (dec) K1, skpo, k19, k19, k2tog, k1. (42 sts)

Rnd 30 K42.

Rnd 31 (dec) K1, skpo, k18, k18, k2tog, k1. (40 sts)

Rnd 32 K40.

Divide right side from left side

Rnd 33 (dec) K1, skpo, k3, k2tog, k1, sl next 11 sts from left side onto spare dpn and set aside, sl second set of 11 sts from back left side onto another dpn and set aside, k1, skpo, k3, k2tog, k1. (14 sts on ndl)

Join in the rnd.

Complete right side

Rnd 34 K14.

Rnd 35 (dec) K4, k2tog, k1, k1, skpo, k4. (12 sts)

Rnd 36 K12.

Rnd 37 K1, kfb, k1, k2tog, k1, k1, skpo, k1, kfb, k1.

Rep last 2 rnds 8 times.

Rnd 54 (inc) Kfb, k1, m1, k2, m1, k1, kfb, kfb, k1, m1, k2, m1, k1, kfb. (20 sts)

Rnd 55 K20.

Rnd 56 (inc) Kfb, k1, m1, k6, m1, k1, kfb, kfb, k1, m1, k6, m1, k1, kfb. (28 sts)

Rnd 57 K28.

Rep last rnd 3 times.

Cut yarn leaving a tail end 5 times the length of sts on one ndl.

Interim sew up

Stuff right side of letter through opening. Close seam by holding the two sets of 14 sts parallel in your left hand, thread cut yarn end into sewing ndl, work Kitchener stitch (see Techniques) to close seam.

Left side

Rnds 33–53 K22.

Rnd 54 (inc) Kfb, k1, m1, k7, m1, k1, kfb, kfb, k1, m1, k7, m1, k1, kfb. (30 sts)

Rnd 55 K30.

Rnd 56 (inc) Kfb, k1, m1, k11, m1, k1, kfb, kfb, k1, m1, k11, m1, k1, kfb. (38 sts)

Rnd 57 K38.

Rep last rnd 3 times.

Cut yarn leaving a tail end 5 times the length of sts on one ndl.

TO FINISH OFF

Stuff left side firmly and evenly.

Hold the two sets of 19 sts parallel in your left hand. Thread the cut yarn end with a sewing needle then work Kitchener stitch to close the seam neatly. Weave in tail ends.

K

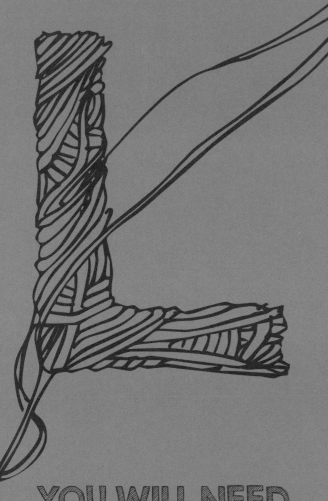

YOU WILL NEED

SMALL
49¼yds (45m) of fingering-weight (4ply) yarn
1 set of 5 dpns size 1 (2.5mm)
2 sets of size 1 (2.5mm) circular needles

MEDIUM
55¾yds (51m) of worsted weight (Aran) yarn
1 set of 5 dpns size 8 (5mm)
2 sets of size 8 (5mm) circular needles

LARGE
109yds (100m) of super-bulky (chunky) yarn
1 set of 5 dpns size 8 (5mm)
2 sets of size 8 (5mm) circular needles

NOTIONS
Blunt-ended tapestry needle
Toy filling
Row counter
2 extra dpns for stitch holders

GAUGE (TENSION)

SMALL 30 sts x 39 rows to 4in (10cm) over st st
MEDIUM 18 sts x 25 rows to 4in (10cm) over st st
LARGE 18 sts x 25 rows to 4in (10cm) over st st

FINISHED SIZE (APPROX)

SMALL 5¼in x 4¼in (13.5cm x 11cm)
MEDIUM 9in x 7½in (23cm x 19cm)
LARGE 15¾in x 13¾in (40cm x 35cm)

YARN CHOICES

Small: Rowan Pure Wool 4ply Jaipur 463 and Rowan Cashsoft 4ply Bluebottle 449

Medium: Rowan Pure Wool Aran Ember 679

Large: (not shown) Rowan Big Wool or any similar weight super-bulky (chunky) yarn

GET KNITTING

Beginning at the bottom of letter working with RS facing work as folls:

Using simple sock cast on method (see Techniques), cast on 64 sts, (32 sts on each ndl).

Rnd 1 K64.

Divide sts equally between 2 circular ndls (32 sts on each ndl), with yarn at tip of RH ndl – have LH sts at top of ndl to be worked. PM.

Rnds 2 & 3 K64.

Rnd 4 (inc) K1, kfb, k30, k30, kfb, k1. (66 sts)

Rnd 5 (inc) Kfb, k32, k32, kfb. (68 sts)

Rnd 6 (dec) K1, kfb, k28, skpo, k2tog, skpo, k2tog, k28, kfb, k1. (66 sts)

Rnd 7 (dec) K1, kfb, k27, skpo, k2tog, skpo, k2tog, k27, kfb, k1. (64 sts)

Shape serif

Work short rows (see Techniques) as folls:

Short row 1 K6, w+t.

Short row 2 P12, w+t.

Short row 3 K11, w+t.

Short row 4 P10, w+t.

Short row 5 K9, w+t.

Short row 6 P8, w+t.

Short row 7 K7, w+t.

Short row 8 P6, w+t.

Short row 9 K5, w+t.

Short row 10 P4, w+t.

Short row 11 K3, w+t.

Short row 12 P2, w+t.

Short row 13 K1.

Cut yarn leaving a tail end twice the length of sts on one ndl.

Using Kitchener stitch (see Techniques) graft together the next 2 sets of 21 sts (42 sts in total), thus leaving 2 sets of 11 sts on ndl.

Left side of letter

With RS facing, rejoin yarn to rem 22 sts.

Join in the rnd.

Rnds 8–53 K22.

Rnd 54 (inc) Kfb, k1, m1, k7, m1, k1, kfb, kfb, k1, m1, k7, m1, k1, kfb. (30 sts)

Rnd 55 K30.

Rnd 56 (inc) Kfb, k1, m1, k11, m1, k1, kfb, kfb, k1, m1, k11, m1, k1, kfb. (38 sts)

Rnd 57 K38.

Rep last rnd 3 times.

Cut yarn leaving a tail end 5 times length of sts on one ndl.

TO FINISH OFF

Stuff the letter firmly and evenly through the opening.

Hold 2 sets of 19 sts parallel in your left hand. Thread cut yarn end with a sewing needle then work Kitchener stitch to close the seam neatly. Weave in tail end.

YOU WILL NEED

SMALL
70yds (64m) of fingering-weight (4ply) yarn
1 set of 5 dpns size 1 (2.5mm)
2 sets of size 1 (2.5mm) circular needles

MEDIUM
98½yds (90m) of worsted weight (Aran) yarn
1 set of 5 dpns size 8 (5mm)
2 sets of size 8 (5mm) circular needles

LARGE
120yds (110m) of super-bulky (chunky) yarn
1 set of 5 dpns size 15 (10mm)
2 sets of size 15 (10mm) circular needles

NOTIONS
Blunt-ended tapestry needle
Toy filling
Row counter
2 extra dpns for stitch holders

GAUGE (TENSION)
SMALL 30 sts x 39 rows to 4in (10cm) over st st
MEDIUM 18 sts x 22 rows to 4in (10cm) over st st
LARGE 7.5 sts x 10 rows to 4in (10cm) over st st

FINISHED SIZE (APPROX)
SMALL 5¼in x 6in (13.5cm x 15cm)
MEDIUM 10¼in 9in (26cm x 23cm)
LARGE 15¾in x 16in (42cm x 40cm)

YARN CHOICES

Small: Rowan Pure Wool 4ply Framboise 456
Medium: Rowan Pure Wool Aran Banana 698
Large: (not shown) Rowan Big Wool or any
similar weight super-bulky (chunky) yarn

GET KNITTING

Top of first and second leg

Working from top with 'M' back to front, cast on 32 sts with simple sock cast on method (see Techniques).

Rnd 1 K32.

Divide sts equally between 2 circular ndls (16 sts on each ndl), with yarn at tip of RH ndl – have LH sts at top of ndl to be worked. PM.

Rnd 2 (inc) K1, m1, k15, k15, m1, k1. (34 sts)

Rnd 3 K34.

Rnd 4 (inc) K1, m1, k16, k16, m1, k1. (36 sts)

Rnd 5 (dec) K14, skpo, k2tog, skpo, k2tog, k14. (32 sts)

Rnd 6 (inc) K1, kfb, k14, k14, kfb, k1. (34 sts)

Rnd 7 (dec) K13, skpo, k2tog, skpo, k2tog, k13. (30 sts)

Rnd 8 (inc) K1, kfb, k13, k13, kfb, k1. (32 sts)

Rnd 9 K32.**

Divide for wider slant (second leg)

Rnd 10 K1, kfb, k8, sl next 6 sts from first leg onto dpn, sl next 6 sts from back first leg onto another dpn, k8, kfb, k1. Set aside dpns. Join rem 22 sts into a rnd and cont as folls:

Rnd 11 K22.

Rnd 12 K1, kfb, k6, k2tog, k1, k1, skpo, k6, kfb, k1.

Rep last 2 rnds 17 times ending with sts at back of second leg.

Cut yarn. Sl two sets of sts onto 2 dpns.

Complete first leg

Rejoin yarn to 12 sts on dpns joining yarn to sts at inner edge. Work with dpns (or spare circulars) as folls:

Rnd 10 K12, join in the rnd.

Rep last rnd 43 times.

Rnd 54 (inc) Kfb, k1, m1, k2, m1, k1, kfb, kfb, k1, m1, k2, m1, k1, kfb. (20 sts)

Rnd 55 K20.

Rnd 56 (inc) Kfb, k1, m1, k6, m1, k1, kfb, kfb, k1, m1, k6, m1, k1, kfb. (28 sts)

Rnd 57 K28.

Rep last rnd 3 times.

Cut yarn leaving a tail end 6 times the length of sts on one ndl. Stuff through the opening.

Hold the two sets of 14 sts parallel in your left hand. Thread cut yarn end with a sewing needle then work Kitchener stitch (see Techniques) to close seam neatly. Weave in tail end.

Top of third and fourth leg

Using simple sock cast on method, cast on 32 sts and work as for first and second leg to **.

Divide for narrow slant (third leg)

Rnd 10 K1, kfb, k3, sl next 11 sts from fourth leg onto a dpn, onto another dpn sl next 11 sts from back fourth leg, k3, kfb, k1. Join rem 12 sts into a rnd. Set aside dpns. Join rem 12 sts into a rnd and cont as folls:

Rnd 11 K12.

Rnd 12 (dec) K1, kfb, k1, k2tog, k1, k1, skpo, k1, kfb, k1.

Rep last 2 rnds 16 times.

Rnd 45 K12, drop marker.

Join together to make V

Rnd 46 K1, kfb, k1, k2tog, k1 (across front of third leg), k1, skpo, k1, kfb, k1 (across back of third leg) onto same ndl k11 from back of second leg (17 sts on ndl), sl 11 sts from front of second leg onto second ndl, k11, then k6 across front of third leg (17 sts on ndl) PM. (34 sts)

Rnd 47 (dec) K1, skpo, k11, k2tog, k1, k1, skpo, k11, k2tog, k1. (30 sts)

Rnd 48 K30.

Rnd 49 (dec) K1, skpo, k9, k2tog, k1, k1, skpo, k9, k2tog, k1. (26 sts)

Rnd 50 K26.

Rnd 51 (dec) K1, skpo, k7, k2tog, k1, k1, skpo, k7, k2tog, k1. (22 sts)

Rnd 52 K22.

Rnd 53 (dec) K1, skpo, k5, k2tog, k1, k1, skpo, k5, k2tog, k1. (18 sts)

Rnd 54 K18.

Stuff through the opening.

Rnd 55 (dec) K1, skpo, k3, k2tog, k1, k1, skpo, k3, k2tog, k1. (14 sts)

Rnd 56 K14.

Rnd 57 (dec) K1, skpo, k1, k2tog, k1, k1, skpo, k1, k2tog, k1. (10 sts)

Rnd 58 (dec) Skpo, k1, k2tog, skpo, k1, k2tog. (6 sts)

Cut yarn, thread end through rem 6 sts, pull up tight to close gap and weave in end to secure.

Complete fourth leg

Rejoin yarn to 22 sts on dpns for fourth leg using circular ndls if easier.

Rnd 10 K22. Join in the rnd.

Rep last rnd 43 times.

Rnd 54 (inc) Kfb, k1, m1, k7, m1, k1, kfb, kfb, k1, m1, k7, m1, k1, kfb. (30 sts)

Rnd 55 K30.

Rnd 56 (inc) Kfb, k1, m1, k11, m1, k1, kfb, kfb, k1, m1, k11, m1, k1, kfb. (38 sts)

Rnd 57 K38.

Cut yarn leaving a tail end 6 times the length of sts on one ndl.

TO FINISH OFF

Stuff letter firmly and evenly.

Hold two sets of 19 sts parallel in your left hand. Thread the cut yarn end with a sewing needle then work Kitchener stitch to close the seam neatly. Weave in tail ends.

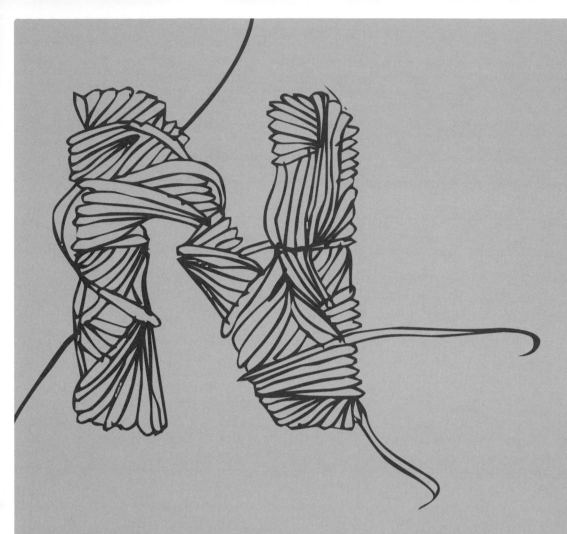

YOU WILL NEED

SMALL
61¼yds (56m) of fingering-weight (4ply) yarn
1 set of 5 dpns size 1 (2.5mm)
2 sets of size 1 (2.5mm) circular needles

MEDIUM
98½yds (90m) of worsted weight (Aran) yarn
1 set of 5 dpns size 8 (5mm)
2 sets of size 8 (5mm) circular needles

LARGE
109yds (100m) of super-bulky (chunky) yarn
1 set of 5 dpns size 15 (10mm)
2 sets of size 15 (10mm) circular needles)

NOTIONS
Blunt-ended tapestry needle
2 extra dpns for stitch holders
Toy filling
Row counter

GAUGE (TENSION)
SMALL 30 sts x 39 rows to 4in (10cm) over st st
MEDIUM 18 sts x 22 rows to 4in (10cm) over st st
LARGE 7.5 sts x 10 rows to 4in (10cm) over st st

FINISHED SIZE (APPROX)
SMALL 5¼in x 4¾in (13.5cm x 12cm)
MEDIUM 10¼in x 7½in (26cm x 19cm)
LARGE 15¾in x 13¾in (40cm x 35cm)

YARN CHOICES

Small: Rowan Pure Wool 4ply Cherish
453 and Eau de Nil 450

Medium: Rowan Pure Wool Aran Mid Indigo 694

Large: (not shown) Rowan Big Wool or any
similar weight super-bulky (chunky) yarn

GET KNITTING

Third leg

Beginning at top of third leg, with RS facing using simple sock cast on method (see Techniques), cast on 28 sts.

Rnd 1 K28.

Divide sts equally between 2 circular ndls (14 sts on each ndl), with yarn at tip of RH ndl – have LH sts at top of ndl to be worked. PM.

Rnds 2–4 K28.

Rnd 5 (dec) Skpo, k2tog, k6, skpo, k2tog, skpo, k2tog, k6, skpo, k2tog. (20 sts)

Rnd 6 K20.

Rnd 7 (dec) Skpo, k2tog, k2, skpo, k2tog, skpo, k2tog, k2, skpo, k2tog. (12 sts)

Rnd 8 K12.

Rep last rnd 29 times.

Cut yarn and sl two sets of sts onto 2 dpns and set aside.

First and second legs

Working rem of letter from top with RS facing.

Using simple sock cast on method, cast on 32 sts.

Rnd 1 K32.

Divide sts equally between 2 circular ndls (16 sts on each ndl), with yarn at tip of RH ndl – have LH sts at top of ndl to be worked. PM.

Rnd 2 (inc) K1, m1, k15, k15, m1, k1. (34 sts)

Rnd 3 K34.

Rnd 4 (inc) K1, m1, k16, k16, m1, k1. (36 sts)

Rnd 5 (dec) K14, skpo, k2tog, skpo, k2tog, k14. (32 sts)

Rnd 6 (inc) K1, kfb, k14, k14, kfb, k1. (34 sts)

Rnd 7 (dec) K13, skpo, k2tog, skpo, k2tog, k13. (30 sts)

Rnd 8 (inc) K1, kfb, k13, k13, kfb, k1. (32 sts)

Rnd 9 K32.

Divide for wider slant - second leg

Rnd 10 K1. kfb, k8 sl next 6 sts from first leg onto a dpn, onto another dpn sl next 6 sts from back of first leg. Set aside both dpns, k8, kfb, k1. (22 sts)

Rnd 11 K22.

Rnd 12 K1, kfb, k6, k2tog, k1, k1, skpo, k6, kfb, k1.

Rep last 2 rnds 12 times.

Cut yarn. Sl 2 sets of sts onto 2 dpns.

Complete first leg

Rejoin yarn to rem 12 sts for first leg, join yarn to sts just after the cut yarn. Working with dpns or spare circular ndls, cont as folls:

Rnd 10 K12.

Join in the rnd.

Rep last rnd 43 times.

Rnd 54 (inc) Kfb, k1, m1, k2, m1, k1, kfb, kfb, k1, m1, k2, m1, k1, kfb. (20 sts)

Rnd 55 K20.

Rnd 56 (inc) Kfb, k1, m1, k6, m1, k1, kfb, kfb, k1, m1, k6, m1, k1, kfb. (28 sts)

Rnd 57 K28.

Rep last rnd 3 times.

Cut yarn leaving a tail end 6 times the length of sts on one ndl.

Stuff letter through opening.

Hold two sets of 14 sts parallel in your left hand. Thread cut yarn end with a sewing needle and work Kitchener stitch (see Techniques) to close seam neatly. Weave in tail end.

Join wider second leg to third leg

Have both second (slanted) and third (straight end) legs of letter with RS facing

Sl front sts from both legs onto one circular ndl and back sts from both legs onto another. WS of letter facing. Rejoin yarn.

Rnd 37 K34.

Join in the rnd.

Rnd 38 (dec) K14, k2tog, k1, k1, skpo, k14. (32 sts)

Rnd 39 K32.

Rnd 40 (dec) K13, k2tog, k1, k1, skpo, k13. (30 sts)

Rnd 41 K30.

Rnds 42–59 Cont as last 2 rnds, dec at end of each side on every alt rnd until 12 sts rem (6 sts on each ndl).

Rnd 60 K3, k2tog, k1, k1, skpo, k3. (10 sts)

Cut yarn, leaving a tail end 5 times the length of sts on one ndl.

TO FINISH OFF

Stuff letter firmly and evenly.

Hold 2 sets of 6 sts parallel in your left hand. Thread cut yarn end with a sewing needle then work Kitchener stitch to close the seam neatly. Weave in tail ends.

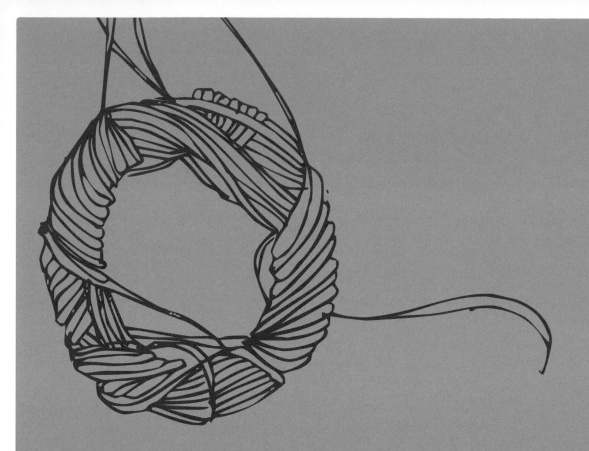

YOU WILL NEED

SMALL
38¼yds (35m) if fingering-weight (4ply) yarn
1 set of 5 dpns size 1 (2.5mm)
2 sets of size 1 (2.5mm) circular needles

MEDIUM
104yds (95m) of worsted weight (Aran) yarn
1 set of 5 dpns size 8 (5mm)
2 sets of size 8 (5mm) circular needles

LARGE
120yds (110m) of super-bulky (chunky) yarn
1 set of 5 dpns size 15 (10mm)
2 sets of size 15 (10mm) circular needles

NOTIONS
Blunt-ended tapestry needle
Toy filling
Row counter
2 extra dpns for stitch holders

GAUGE (TENSION)
SMALL 30 sts x 39 rows to 4in (10cm) over st st
MEDIUM 18 sts x 25 rows to 4in (10cm) over st st
LARGE 7.5 sts x 10 rows to 4in (10cm) over st st

FINISHED SIZE (APPROX)
SMALL 5¼in x 4¼in (13.5cm x 11cm)
MEDIUM 9¾in x 9in (24cm x 23cm)
LARGE 15¾in x 12¼in (42cm x 31cm)

YARN CHOICES

Small: Rowan Pure Wool Jaipur 463, Cherish 453, Vintage 449 and Avocado 419

Medium: Rowan Pure Wool Aran Splash 701 and Ivory 670

Large: (not shown) Rowan Big Wool or any similar weight super-bulky (chunky) yarn

GET KNITTING

Beginning at the bottom of letter working upside down and with WS facing cont as folls:

Using simple sock cast on method (see Techniques), cast on 38 sts, (19 sts on each ndl).

Rnd 1 (inc) K1, kfb, k15, kfb, k1, k1, kfb, k15, kfb, k1. (42 sts)

Divide sts equally between 2 circular ndls (21 sts on each ndl), with yarn at tip of RH ndl – have LH sts at top of ndl to be worked. PM.

Rnd 2 K42.

Rnd 3 (inc) K1, kfb, k17, kfb, k1, k1, kfb, k17, kfb, k1. (46 sts)

Rnd 4 K46.

Rnd 5 (inc) K1, kfb, k19, kfb, k1, k1, kfb, k19, kfb, k1. (50 sts)

Rnd 6 K50.

Rnd 7 (inc) K1, kfb, k21, kfb, k1, k1, kfb, k21, kfb, k1. (54 sts)

Rnd 8 K54.

Create hole in centre

Rnd 9 K1, kfb, k6, k2tog, bind (cast) off 8 sts, k6, kfb, k1, k1, kfb, k6, k2tog, bind (cast) off 8 sts, k6, kfb, k1.

Right side

Rnd 10 K10, sl next 10 sts off circular ndl and onto a dpn and set aside. Sl next 10 sts off circular ndl and onto another dpn and set aside, k10 for back of right side, working on these 20 sts only join in rnd and cont as folls:

Rnd 11 (inc) K1, kfb, k8, k8, kfb, k1. (22 sts)

Rnds 12 & 13 K22.

Rnd 14 K1, kfb, k6, k2tog, k1, k1, skpo, k6, kfb, k1.

Rnds 15 &16 K22.

Rnd 17 K1, kfb, k9, k9, kfb, k1. (24 sts)

Rnd 18 K24.

Rnd 19 K1, kfb, k7, k2tog, k1, k1, skpo, k7, kfb, k1.

Rnds 20–41 K24.

Rnd 42 K1, skpo, k7, kfb, k1, k1, kfb, k7, k2tog, k1.

Rnd 43 K24.

Rnd 44 (dec) K1, skpo, k9, k9, k2tog, k1. (22 sts)

Rnds 45 & 46 K22.

Rnd 47 K1, skpo, k6, kfb, k1, k1, kfb, k6, k2tog, k1.

Rnds 48 & 49 K22.

Rnd 50 (dec) K1, skpo, k8, k8, k2tog, k1. (20 sts)

Rnd 51 K20.

Rnd 52 (inc) K1, skpo, k5, kfb, k1, turn so that WS (p side) is facing, cast on 4 sts, p15, p2tog, p5, kfb, p1, turn, cast on 4 sts. (28 sts)

Work in rows

Cont backwards and forwards in rows as folls:

Next row K28.

Next row (dec) P11, p2tog tbl, p1, p1, p2tog, p11. (26 sts)

Next row K26.

Next row (dec) P10, p2tog tbl, p1, p1, p2tog, p10. (24 sts)

Next row K24.

Next row (dec) P9, p2tog tbl, p1, p1, p2tog, p9. (22 sts)

Next row K22.

Next row (dec) P7, p2tog tbl, p1, p1, p2tog, p7. (20 sts)

Cut yarn leaving a tail end 6 times the length of the sts on one ndl.

Hold the two sets of 10 sts parallel in your left hand. Thread cut yarn end with a sewing needle then work Kitchener stitch (see Techniques) to close the seam. Weave in tail end.

Left side

Rejoin yarn to rem 2 sets of sts from left side at inner edge just after bind (cast) off, working with dpns (or spare circulars), cont as folls:

Rnd 10 (inc) K8, kfb, k1, k1, kfb, k8. (22 sts)

Join in the rnd.

Rnds 11 & 12 K22.

Rnd 13 K1, skpo, k6, kfb, k1, k1, kfb, k6, k2tog, k1.

Rnds 14 & 15 K22.

Rnd 16 (inc) K9, kfb, k1, k1, kfb, k9. (24 sts)

Rnd 17 K24.

Rnd 18 K1, skpo, k7, kfb, k1, k1, kfb, k7, k2tog, k1.

Rnds 19–41 K24.

Rnd 42 K1, skpo, k7, kfb, k1, k1, kfb, k7, k2tog, k1.

Rnd 43 K24.

Rnd 44 (dec) K9, k2tog, k1, k1, skpo, k9. (22 sts)

Rnds 45 & 46 K22.

Rnd 47 K1, skpo, k6, kfb, k1, k1, kfb, k6, k2tog, k1.

Rnds 48 & 49 K22.

Rnd 50 (inc) K8, k2tog, k1, k1, skpo, k8. (20 sts)

Rnd 51 K20.

Rnd 52 (inc) Cast on 4 sts, k5, kfb, k5, k2tog, k1, k1, skpo, k5, kfb, k1, turn so that WS (p side) is facing, cast on 4 sts, p28.

Work in rows

Cont backwards and forwards in rows as folls:

Next row (dec) K11, k2tog, k1, k1, skpo, k11. (26 sts)

Next row P26.

Next row (dec) K10, k2tog, k1, k1, skpo, k10. (24 sts)

Next row P24.

Next row (dec) K9, k2tog, k1, k1, skpo, k9. (22 sts)

Next row P22.

Next row (dec) K8, k2tog, k1, k1, skpo, k8. (20 sts)

Cut yarn leaving a tail end 6 times the length of the sts on one ndl.

TO FINISH OFF

Hold 2 sets of 10 sts parallel in your left hand. Thread cut yarn end with a sewing needle then work Kitchener stitch to close the seam neatly.

Join the seven rows ends to join the bottom of the letter neatly with mattress seam. Stuff the letter firmly and evenly through the opening. Close the opening with mattress seam. Weave in tail ends.

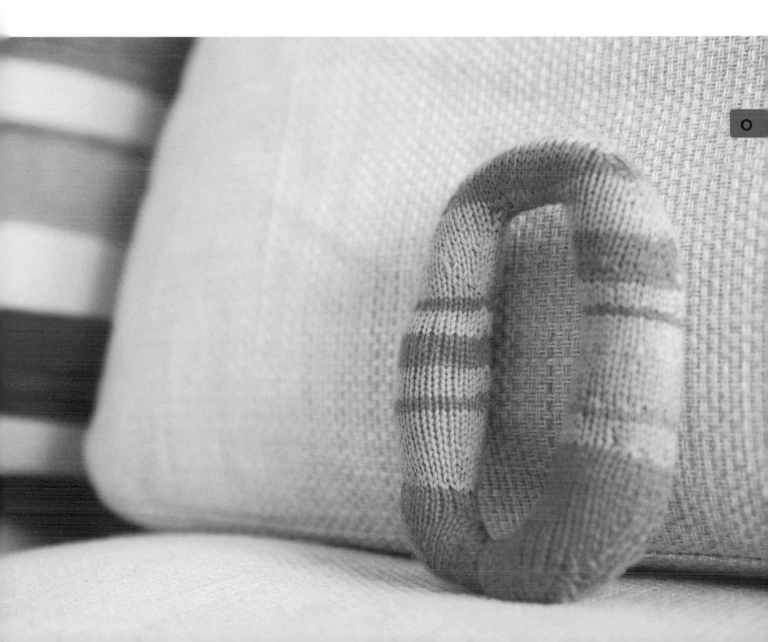

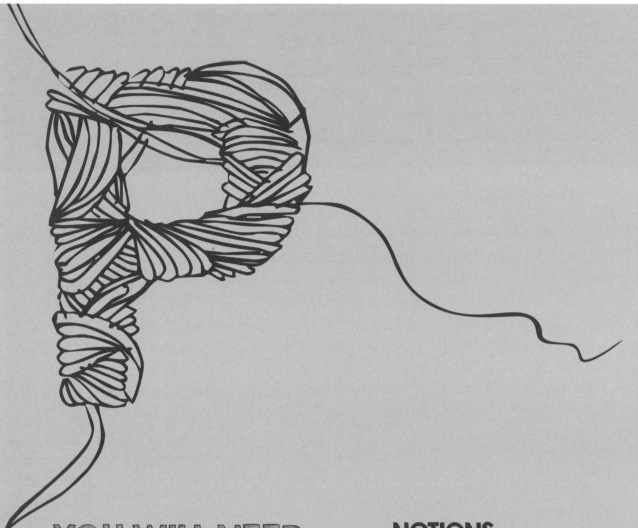

YOU WILL NEED

SMALL
44yds (40m) of fingering-weight (4ply) yarn
1 set of 5 dpns size 1 (2.5mm)
2 sets of size 1 (2.5mm) circular needles

MEDIUM
66yds (60m) of worsted weight (Aran) yarn
1 set of 5 dpns size 8 (5mm)
2 sets of size 8 (5mm) circular needles

LARGE
109yds (100m) of super-bulky (chunky) yarn
1 set of 5 dpns size 15 (10mm)
2 sets of size 15 (10mm) circular needles

NOTIONS
Blunt-ended tapestry needle
Toy filling
Row counter

GAUGE (TENSION)
SMALL 30 sts x 39 rows to 4in (10cm) over st st
MEDIUM 18 sts x 25 rows to 4in (10cm) over st st
LARGE 7.5 sts x 10 rows to 4in (10cm) over st st

FINISHED SIZE (APPROX)
SMALL 5½in x 4in (14cm x 10cm)
MEDIUM 9½in x 7¾in (24cm x 17cm)
LARGE 15¾in x 13¾in (40cm x 35cm)

YARN CHOICES

Small: Rowan Pure Wool 4ply Vintage 449

Medium: Rowan Pure Wool Aran Banana 698

Large: (not shown) Rowan Big Wool or any similar weight super-bulky (chunky) yarn

GET KNITTING

Top of letter

Working with letter upside down and back to front, using simple sock cast on method (see Techniques), cast on 52 sts.

Rnd 1 K52.

Divide sts equally between 2 circular ndls (26 sts on each ndl), with yarn at tip of RH ndl – have LH sts at top of ndl to be worked. PM.

Rnd 2 (inc) K1, kfb, k24, k24, kfb, k1. (54 sts)

Rnd 3 (dec) Kfb, k21, skpo, k2tog, k1, k1, skpo, k2tog, k21, kfb. (52 sts)

Rnd 4 (inc) K1, kfb, k24, k24, kfb, k1. (54 sts)

Rnd 5 (dec) Kfb, k21, skpo, k2tog, k1, k1, skpo, k2tog, k21, kfb. (52 sts)

Rep last 2 rnds once.

Rnd 8 (inc) K1, kfb, k24, k24, kfb, k1. (54 sts)

Divide straight from curved side

Rnd 9 K1, kfb, k6, k2tog, bind (cast) off 6 sts, k10, k11 bind (cast) off 7 sts, k6, kfb, k1.

Curved side

Rnd 10 K10, sl next 11 sts off circular needle and onto a dpn, sl next 11 sts onto another dpn, k10 for back of curved side and cont on these 20 sts as folls:

Rnd 11 (inc) K1, kfb, k8, k8, kfb, k1. (22 sts)

Rnds 12 & 13 K22.

Rnd 14 K1, kfb, k6, k2tog, k1, k1, skpo, k6, kfb, k1.

Rnd 15 K22.

Rep last rnd 6 times.

Rnd 22 K1, skpo, k6, kfb, k1, k1, kfb, k6, k2tog, k1.

Rnds 23 & 24 K22.

Rnd 25 (dec) K1, skpo, k8, k8, k2tog, k1. (20 sts)

Rnd 26 K20.

Set aside these 20 sts and return to rem sts.

Straight side

Rejoin yarn to 22 sts from straight side joining yarn to inner edge. Working with dpns (or spare circulars), cont as folls:

Rnd 9 K22. Join in the rnd.

Rep last rnd 17 times.

Cut yarn.

Join curved side with straight side

Return to curved side and work across first 10 sts, shaping as folls:

Rnd 26 (inc) K1, skpo, k5, kfb, k1, backward loop cast on 4 sts, k across first set of 11 sts from straight side (25 sts on one ndl), sl second set of 11 sts from straight side onto the other circular ndl then k these sts, backward loop cast on 4 sts, k across rem sts from curved side shaping as folls: k1, kfb, k5, k2tog, k1 (25 sts on second ndl). Join in the rnd.

Rnd 27 K50.

Rnd 28 (dec) K1, skpo, k22, k22, k2tog, k1. (48 sts)

Rnd 29 K48.

Rnd 30 (dec) K1, skpo, k21, k21, k2tog, k1. (46 sts)

Rnd 31 K46.

Rnd 32 (dec) K1, skpo, k20, k20, k2tog, k1. (44 sts)

Rnd 33 K44.

Rnd 34 (dec) K1, skpo, k19, k19, k2tog, k1. (42 sts)

Cut yarn leaving a tail end 3 times the length of sts on one needle.

Sew up seam

Hold the two sets of 21 sts held parallel in your left hand, work Kitchener stitch (see Techniques) over next 10 pairs of sts only, to close the seam under the curve neatly. Weave in tail end.

Finish straight side

Cont on rem sts from straight side.

Rnd 35 K22.

Join in the rnd.

Rep last rnd 18 times.

Rnd 54 (inc) Kfb, k1, m1, k7, m1, k1, kfb, kfb, k1, m1, k7, m1, k1, kfb. (30 sts)

Rnd 55 K30.

Rnd 56 (inc) Kfb, k1, m1, k11, m1, k1, kfb, kfb, k1, m1, k11, m1, k1, kfb. (38 sts)

Rnd 57 K38.

Rep last rnd 3 times.

Cut yarn leaving a tail end 5 times the length of sts on one ndl.

TO FINISH OFF

Hold the two sets of 19 sts parallel in your left hand. Thread the cut yarn end with a sewing needle then work Kitchener stitch to close the seam neatly. Stuff letter firmly and evenly through openings.

Close seams with mattress stitch. Weave in tail ends.

P

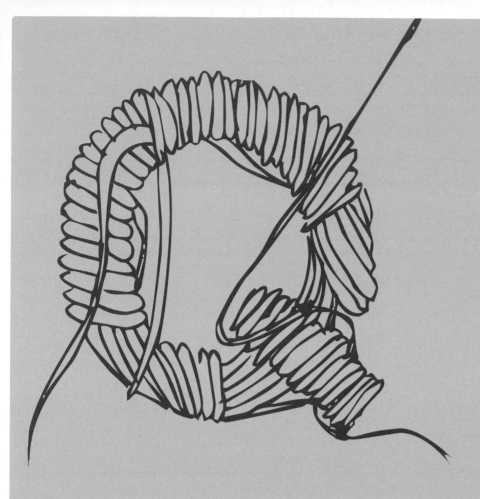

YOU WILL NEED

SMALL

43yds (39m) of fingering-weight (4ply) yarn
1 set of 5 dpns size 1 (2.5mm)
2 sets of size 1 (2.5mm) circular needles

MEDIUM

90yds (82m) of worsted (Aran) yarn
1 set of 5 dpns size 8 (5mm)
2 sets of size 8 (5mm) circular needles

LARGE

164yds (150m) of super-bulky (chunky) yarn
1 set of 5 dpns size 15 (10mm)
2 sets of size 15 (10mm) circular needles

NOTIONS

Blunt-ended tapestry needle
Toy filling
Row counter

GAUGE (TENSION)

SMALL 30 sts x 39 rows to 4in (10cm) over st st
MEDIUM 18 sts x 25 rows to 4in (10cm) over st st
LARGE 7.5 sts x 10 rows to 4in (10cm) over st st

FINISHED SIZE (APPROX)

SMALL 6in x 4in (15cm x 10cm)
MEDIUM 9in x 6¾in (23cm x 17cm)
LARGE 20½in x 12¼in (52cm x 31cm)

YARN CHOICES...

Small: (not shown) Rowan Pure Wool
4ply Eau de Nil 450 and Shale 402

Medium: (not hown) Rowan Pure Wool Aran
or any similar weight worsted/aran yarn

Large: Rowan Big Wool Zing 037

Q

GET KNITTING

Bottom of letter

Beginning at bottom of letter with RS facing, cast on 22 sts using simple sock cast on method (see Techniques).

Rnd 1 K1, skpo, k6, kfb, k1, k1, kfb, k6, k2tog, k1.

Divide sts equally between 2 circular ndls (11 sts on each ndl), with yarn at tip of RH ndl – have LH sts at top of ndl to be worked. PM.

Rnd 2 K22.

Rnd 3 (inc) K1, skpo, k6, m1, k1, kfb, kfb, k1, m1, k6, k2tog, k1. (24 sts)

Rnd 4 K24.

Rnd 5 (inc) K1, skpo, k7, m1, k1, kfb, kfb, k1, m1, k7, k2tog, k1. (26 sts)

Rnd 6 K26.

Rnd 7 (inc) K1, skpo, k8, m1, k1, kfb, kfb, k1, m1, k8, k2tog, k1. (28 sts)

Rnd 8 K28.

Rnd 9 (inc) K1, skpo, k9, m1, k1, kfb, kfb, k1, m1, k9, k2tog, k1. (30 sts)

Rnd 10 K30.

Rnd 11 (inc) K1, skpo, k10, m1, k1, kfb, kfb, k1, m1, k10, k2tog, k1. (32 sts)

Rnd 12 K32.

Rnd 13 (inc) K1, kfb, k12, m1, k1, kfb, kfb, k1, m1, k12, kfb, k1. (38 sts)

Rnd 14 K38.

Rnd 15 (inc) K1, kfb, k15, kfb, k1, k1, kfb, k15, kfb, k1. (42 sts)

Rnd 16 K42.

Rnd 17 (inc) K1, kfb, k17, kfb, k1, k1, kfb, k17, kfb, k1. (46 sts)

Rnd 18 K46.

Rnd 19 (inc) K1, kfb, k19, kfb, k1, k1, kfb, k19, kfb, k1. (50 sts)

Rnd 20 K50.

Rnd 21 (inc) K1, kfb, k21, kfb, k1, k1, kfb, k21, kfb, k1. (54 sts)

Rnd 22 K54.

Create hole in centre

Rnd 23 K1, kfb, k6, k2tog, bind (cast) off 8 sts, k6, kfb, k1, k1, kfb, k6, k2tog, bind (cast) off 8 sts, k6, kfb, k1.

Right side

Rnd 24 K10, sl next 10 sts off circular ndl and onto a dpn and set aside, sl next 10 sts off circular and onto another dpn and set aside, k10, 20 sts for each side of the letter.

Rnd 25 (inc) K1, kfb, k8, k8, kfb, k1. (22 sts)

Join in the rnd.

Rnds 26 & 27 K22.

Rnd 28 K1, kfb, k6, k2tog, k1, k1, skpo, k6, kfb, k1.

Rnds 29 & 30 K22.

Rnd 31 (inc) K1, kfb, k9, k9, kfb, k1. (24 sts)

Rnd 32 K24.

Rnd 33 K1, kfb, k7, k2tog, k1, k1, skpo, k7, kfb, k1.

Rnds 34–55 K24.

Rnd 56 K1, kfb, k7, k2tog, k1, k1, skpo, k7, kfb, k1.

Rnd 57 K24.

Rnd 58 (dec) K1, skpo, k9, k9, k2tog, k1. (22 sts)

Rnds 59 & 60 K22.

Rnd 61 K1, skpo, k6, kfb, k1, k1, kfb, k6, k2tog, k1.

Rnds 62 & 63 K22.

Rnd 64 (dec) K1, skpo, k8, k8, k2tog, k1. (20 sts)

Rnd 65 K20.

Rnd 66 (inc) K1, skpo, k5, kfb, k1, turn so that WS (p side) is facing, backwards loop cast on 4 sts, p15, p2tog, p5, kfb, p1, turn, cast on 4 sts. (28 sts)

Work in rows

Cont backwards and forwards in rows as folls:

Next row K28.

Next row (dec) P11, p2tog, p1, p1, p2tog, p11. (26 sts)

Next row K26.

Next row (dec) P10, p2tog, p1, p1, p2tog, p10. (24 sts)

Next row K24.

Next row (dec) P9, p2tog, p1, p1, p2tog, p9. (22 sts)

Next row K22.

Next row (dec) P7, p2tog, p1, p1, p2tog, p7. (20 sts)

Cut yarn leaving a tail end 6 times the length of sts on one ndl.

Hold the two sets of 10 sts parallel in your left hand. Thread cut yarn end with a sewing needle then work Kitchener stitch (see Techniques) to close seam neatly. Weave in tail end.

Left side

With RS of letter facing rejoin yarn to rem 2 sets of sts from left side at inner edge just after cast off, working with dpns (or spare circulars), cont as folls:

Rnd 24 (inc) K8, kfb, k1, k1, kfb, k8. (22 sts)

Join in the rnd.

Rnds 25 & 26 K22.

Rnd 27 K1, skpo, k6, kfb, k1, k1, kfb, k6, k2tog, k1.

Rnds 28 & 29 K22.

Rnd 30 (inc) K9, kfb, k1, k1, kfb, k9. (24 sts)

Rnd 31 K24.

Rnd 32 K1, skpo, k7, kfb, k1, k1, kfb, k7, k2tog, k1.

Rnds 33–55 K24.

Rnd 56 K1, skpo, k7, kfb, k1, k1, kfb, k7, k2tog, k1.

Rnd 57 K24.

Rnd 58 (dec) K9, k2tog, k1, k1, skpo, k9. (22 sts)

Rnds 59 & 60 K22.

Rnd 61 K1, skpo, k6, kfb, k1, k1, kfb, k6, k2tog, k1.

Rnds 62 & 63 K22.

Rnd 64 (dec) K8, k2tog, k1, k1, skpo, k8. (20 sts)

Rnd 65 K20.

Rnd 66 (inc) Cast on 4 sts, k5, kfb, k5, k2tog, k1, k1, skpo, k5, kfb, k1, turn so that WS (p side) is facing, backwards loop cast on 4 sts, p28.

Work in rows

Cont backwards and forwards in rows as folls:

Next row (dec) K11, k2tog, k1, k1, skpo, k11. (26 sts)

Next row P26.

Next row (dec) K10, k2tog, k1, k1, skpo, k10. (24 sts)

Next row P24.

Next row (dec) K9, k2tog, k1, k1, skpo, k9. (22 sts)

Next row P22.

Next row (dec) K8, k2tog, k1, k1, skpo, k8. (20 sts)

Cut yarn leaving a tail end 5 times the length of sts on one ndl.

Hold the two sets of 10 sts parallel in your left hand. Thread the cut yarn end with a sewing needle then work Kitchener stitch to close the seam neatly. Weave in the tail end.

TO FINISH OFF

Join the seven rows ends to the bottom of the letter neatly with mattress stitch.

Stuff the letter firmly and evenly. Close seams with mattress stitch.

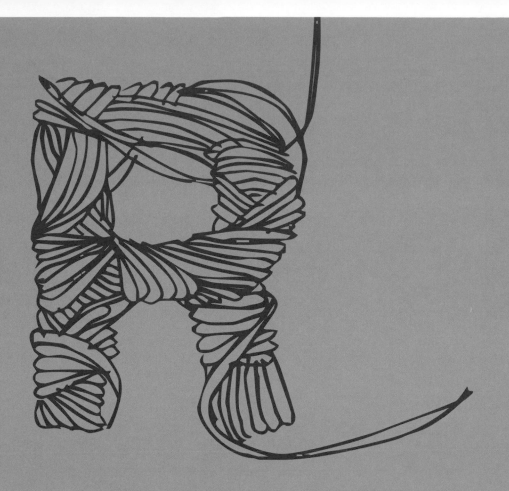

YOU WILL NEED

SMALL
40½yds (37m) of fingering-weight (4ply) yarn
1 set of 5 dpns size 1 (2.5mm)
2 sets of size 1 (2.5mm) circular needles

MEDIUM
110yds (100m) of worsted weight (Aran) yarn
1 set of 5 dpns size 8 (5mm)
2 sets of size 8 (5mm) circular needles

LARGE
109yds (100m) of super-bulky (chunky) yarn
1 set of 5 dpns size 15 (10mm)
2 sets of size 15 (10mm) circular needles

NOTIONS
Blunt-ended tapestry needle
Toy filling
Row counter
2 extra dpns for stitch holders

GAUGE (TENSION)
SMALL 30 sts x 39 rows to 4in (10cm) over st st
MEDIUM 18 sts x 25 rows to 4in (10cm) over st st
LARGE 7.5 sts x 10 rows to 4in (10cm) over st st

FINISHED SIZE (APPROX)
SMALL 5¼in x 4¼in (13.5cm x 11cm)
MEDIUM 9¾in x 7in (25cm x 18cm)
LARGE 15¾ x 13¾in (40cm x 35cm)

YARN CHOICES

Small: Patons Diploma Gold 4ply
shade Delphinium 04299

Medium: Rowan Creative Focus
Worsted Deep Rose 2755

Large: (not shown) Rowan Pure Wool Aran
or any similar weight worsted/aran yarn

R

Top of letter

For small and medium sizes you may need to use two balls of yarn.

Beginning at the top and working with letter upside down, using simple sock cast on method (see Techniques), cast on 52 sts.

Rnd 1 K52.

Divide sts equally between 2 circular ndls (26 sts on each ndl), with yarn at tip of RH ndl – have LH sts at top of ndl to be worked. PM.

Rnd 2 (inc) K1, kfb, k24, k24, kfb, k1. (54 sts)

Rnd 3 (dec) Kfb, k21, skpo, k2tog, k1, k1, skpo, k2tog, k21, kfb. (52 sts)

Rnd 4 (inc) K1, kfb, k24, k24, kfb, k1. (54 sts)

Rnd 5 (dec) Kfb, k21, skpo, k2tog, k1, k1, skpo, k2tog, k21, kfb. (52 sts)

Rep last 2 rnds once.

Rnd 8 (inc) K1, kfb, k24, k24, kfb, k1. (54 sts)

Divide straight from curved side

Rnd 9 K1, kfb, k6, k2tog, bind (cast) off 6 sts, k10, k11 bind (cast) off 7 sts, k6, kfb, k1.

Curved side

Rnd 10 K10, sl next 11 sts off circular needle and onto a dpn, sl next 11 sts onto another dpn, k10 for back of curved side and cont on these 20 sts as folls:

Rnd 11 (inc) K1, kfb, k8, k8, kfb, k1. (22 sts)

Rnds 12 & 13 K22.

Rnd 14 K1, kfb, k6, k2tog, k1, k1, skpo, k6, kfb, k1.

Rnd 15 K22.

Rep last rnd 6 times.

Rnd 22 K1, skpo, k6, kfb, k1, k1, kfb, k6, k2tog, k1.

Rnds 23 & 24 K22.

Rnd 25 (dec) K1, skpo, k8, k8, k2tog, k1. (20 sts)

Rnd 26 K20.

Set aside these 20 sts and return to rem sts.

Straight side

Rejoin yarn to 22 sts from straight side joining yarn to inner edge. Working with dpns (or spare circulars), cont as folls:

Rnd 9 K22. Join in the rnd.

Rep last rnd 17 times. Cut yarn.

Join curved side with straight side

Return to curved side and work across first 10 sts, shaping as folls:

Rnd 27 (inc) K1, skpo, k5, kfb, k1, backward loop cast on 4 sts, k across first set of 11 sts from straight side (25 sts on one ndl), sl second set of 11 sts from straight side onto the other circular ndl then k these sts, backward loop cast on 4 sts, k across rem sts from curved side shaping as folls: k1, kfb, k5, k2tog, k1 (25 sts on second ndl). Join in the rnd.

Rnd 28 K50.

Rnd 29 (dec) K1, skpo, k22, k22, k2tog, k1. (48 sts)

Rnd 30 K48.

Shape slope

Rnd 31 (dec) K1, skpo, k9, sl next 12 sts off circular ndl and onto dpn, sl next 12 sts onto another dpn, k9, k2tog, k1 for back of slope.

Set aside dpns and cont on 2 sets of 11 sts only.

Rnd 32 K1, kfb, k6, k2tog, k1, k1, skpo, k6, kfb, k1.

Rnd 33 Kfb, k8, k2tog, skpo, k8, kfb.

Rep last 2 rnds 10 times.

Rnd 54 K1, kfb, k6, k2tog, k1, k1, skpo, k6, kfb, k1.

Rnd 55 (inc) Kfb, k1, m1, k7, k2tog, skpo, k7, m1, k1, kfb. (24 sts)

Rnd 56 K24.

Rnd 57 (inc) Kfb, k1, m1, k7, k2tog, k1, k1, skpo, k7, m1, k1, kfb. (26 sts)

Rnd 58 K26.

Rep last rnd twice.

Cut yarn leaving a tail end 6 times the length of sts on one needle.

Interim sew up

Stuff right side of the letter then close seam as folls: hold the two sets of 13 sts parallel in your left hand, work Kitchener stitch (see Techniques) to close the seam under the curve neatly. Weave in tail end.

Finish straight side

Rejoin yarn to 24 sts from straight side at the join where slope sts begin. Working with dpns or circular ndls, cont as folls:

Rnd 30 K24.

Rnd 31 (dec) K1, skpo, k9, k9, k2tog, k1. (22 sts)

Rnd 32 K22.

Rep last rnd 21 times.

Rnd 54 (inc) Kfb, k1, m1, k7, m1, k1, kfb, kfb, k1, m1, k7, m1, k1, kfb. (30 sts)

Rnd 55 K30.

Rnd 56 (inc) Kfb, k1, m1, k11, m1, k1, kfb, kfb, k1, m1, k11, m1, k1, kfb. (38 sts)

Rnd 57 K38.

Rep last rnd 3 times.

Cut yarn leaving a tail end 6 times the length of sts on one ndl.

TO FINISH OFF

Stuff letter firmly and evenly.

Hold the two sets of 19 sts parallel in your left hand. Thread the cut yarn end with a sewing needle then work Kitchener stitch to close the seam neatly. Stuff letter firmly and evenly through openings.

Close seams with mattress stitch. Weave in tail ends.

YOU WILL NEED

SMALL
52½yds (48m) of fingering-weight (4ply) yarn
1 set of 5 dpns size 1 (2.5mm)
2 sets of size 1 (2.5mm) circular needles

MEDIUM
98½yds (90m) of worsted weight (Aran) yarn
1 set of 5 dpns size 8 (5mm)
2 sets of size 8 (5mm) circular needles

LARGE
109yds (100m) of super-bulky (chunky) yarn
1 set of 5 dpns size 15 (10mm)
2 sets of size 15 (10mm) circular needles

NOTIONS
Blunt-ended tapestry needle
2 extra dpns for stitch holders
Toy filling
Row counter

GAUGE (TENSION)

SMALL 30 sts x 39 rows to 4in (10cm) over st st

MEDIUM 18 sts x 25 rows to 4in (10cm) over st st

LARGE 7.5 sts x 10 rows to 4in (10cm) over st st

FINISHED SIZE (APPROX)

SMALL 5¼in x 4in (13.5cm x 10cm)

MEDIUM 9in x 7½in (23cm x 19cm)

LARGE 15¾in x 13¾in (40cm x 35cm)

YARN CHOICES

Small: Rowan Pure Wool 4ply Avocado 419
Medium: Rowan Pure Wool Aran Burnt 700
Large: (not shown) Rowan Big Wool or any
similar weight super-bulky (chunky) yarn

Beginning at bottom of letter working downwards with RS facing work as folls:

Using simple sock cast on method (see Techniques), cast on 30 sts, (15 sts on each ndl).

Rnd 1 K30.

Divide sts equally between 2 circular ndls (15 sts on each ndl), with yarn at tip of RH ndl – have LH sts at top of ndl to be worked. PM.

Rnds 2–4 K30.

Rnd 5 (dec) Skpo, k2tog, k7, skpo, k2tog, skpo, k2tog, k7, skpo, k2tog. (22 sts)

Rnd 6 K22.

Rnd 7 (dec) K7, skpo, k2tog, skpo, k2tog, k7. (18 sts)

Rnd 8 K18.

Rnd 9 (dec) K1, skpo, k2, skpo, k2tog, skpo, k2tog, k2, k2tog, k1. (12 sts)

Rnd 10 K12.

Shape first curve

Work short rows (see Techniques) as folls:

Short row 1 *K11, w+t.

Short row 2 P10, w+t.

Short row 3 K9, w+t.

Short row 4 P8, w+t.

Short row 5 K7, w+t.

Short row 6 P6, w+t.

Short row 7 K5, w+t.

Short row 8 P4, w+t.

Short row 9 K3, w+t.

Short row 10 P2, w+t.**

Short row 11 K7 to marker.

Join back into the rnd.

Rnds 11 & 12 K12.

Rnd 13 (inc) K1, kfb, k4, k4, kfb, k1. (14 sts)

Shape second curve

Work short rows as folls:

Short row 1 K13, w+t.

Short row 2 P12, w+t.

Work as for first curve from * to **.

Short row 13 K8 to marker.

Join back into the rnd.

Rnds 14 & 15 K14.

Rnd 16 (inc) K1, kfb, k5, k5, kfb, k1. (16 sts)

Shape third curve

Work short rows as folls:

Short row 1 K15, w+t.

Short row 2 P14, w+t.

Short row 3 K13, w+t.

Short row 4 P12, w+t.

Work as for first curve from * to **.

Short row 15 K9 to marker.

Join back into the rnd.

Rnds 17 & 18 K16.

Rnd 19 (inc) K1, kfb, k6, k6, kfb, k1. (18 sts)

Shape fourth curve

Work short rows as folls:

Short row 1 ***K17, w+t.

Short row 2 P16, w+t.

Short row 3 K15, w+t.

Short row 4 P14, w+t.

Short row 5 K13, w+t.

Short row 6 P12, w+t.

Work as for first curve from * to **.

Short row 17 K10 to marker.

Join back into the rnd.

Rnds 20 & 21 K18.

Rnd 22 (inc) K1, kfb, k7, k7, kfb, k1. (20 sts)

Rnd 23 K20.

Rnd 24 (inc) K1, kfb, k8, k8, kfb, k1. (22 sts)

At this halfway position, begin to stuff the letter firmly. The short row shaping creates small gaps in the knitting so stuff with scraps of same colour yarn as well as toy filling.

The curves will now need to be worked in the opposite direction. To achieve this remove marker, knit next 11 sts then PM for a new beginning of rnd.

Shape fifth curve

Work short rows as folls:

Short row 1 K21, w+t.

Short row 2 P20, w+t.

Short row 3 K19, w+t.

Short row 4 P18, w+t.

Work as for fourth curve from *** to **.

Short row 21 K12 to marker.

Join back into the rnd.

Rnds 25 & 26 K22.

Rnd 27 (dec) K1, skpo, k8, k8, k2tog, k1. (20 sts)

Shape sixth curve

Work short rows as folls:

Short row 1 K19, w+t.

Short row 2 P18, w+t.

Work as for fourth curve from *** to **.

Short row 19 K11, to marker.

Join back into the rnd.

Rnds 28 & 29 K20.

Rnd 30 (dec) K1, skpo, k7, k7, k2tog, k1. (18 sts)

Shape seventh curve

Work as for fourth curve from *** to **.

Short row 17 K10 to marker.

Join back into the rnd.

Rnds 31 & 32 K18.

Rnd 33 (dec) K1, skpo, k6, k6, k2tog, k1. (16 sts)

Shape eighth curve

Work short rows as folls:

Short row 1 K15, w+t.

Short row 2 P14, w+t.

Work as for second curve from **Short row 1** to **.

Short row 15 K9 to marker.

Join back into the rnd.

Rnds 34 & 35 K16.

Rnd 36 (dec) K1, skpo, k5, k5, k2tog, k1. (14 sts)

Remove marker.

Shape ninth curve

Rnd 37 K7. PM.

Work short rows as folls:

Short row 1 K13, w+t.

Short row 2 P12, w+t.

Work as for first curve from * to **.

Short row 13 K8 to marker.

Join back into the rnd.

Rnd 38 K14.

Rnd 39 (inc) Kfb, k1, m1, k3, kfb, k1, k1, kfb, k3, m1, k1, kfb (20 sts)

Rnd 40 K20.

Rnd 41 (inc) K1, kfb, k6, kfb, k1, k1, kfb, k6, kfb, k1. (24 sts)

Rnd 42 K24.

Rnd 43 (inc) Kfb, k1, m1, k8, m1, k1, kfb, kfb, k1, m1, k8, m1, k1, kfb. (32 sts)

Rnd 44 K32.

Rep last rnd 3 times.

Cut yarn leaving a tail end 4 times the length of sts on one ndl.

TO FINISH OFF

Stuff the second half of the letter firmly and evenly joining with Kitchener stitch (see Techniques). Weave in tail end.

S

YOU WILL NEED

SMALL
18½yds (17m) of fingering-weight (4ply) yarn
1 set of 5 dpns size 1 (2.5mm)
2 sets of size 1 (2.5mm) circular needles

MEDIUM
47yds (43m) of worsted weight (Aran) yarn
1 set of 5 dpns size 8 (5mm)
2 sets of size 8 (5mm) circular needles

LARGE
109yds (100m) of super-bulky (chunky) yarn
1 set of 5 dpns size 15 (10mm)
2 sets of size 15 (10mm) circular needles

NOTIONS

Blunt-ended tapestry needle
2 extra dpns for stitch holders
Toy filling
Row counter

GAUGE (TENSION)

SMALL 30 sts x 39 rows to 4in (10cm) over st st
MEDIUM 18 sts x 25 rows to 4in (10cm) over st st
LARGE 7.5 sts x 10 rows to 4in (10cm) over st st

FINISHED SIZE (APPROX)

SMALL 5¼in x 4in (13.5cm x 10cm)
MEDIUM 9in x 6¾in (23cm x 17cm)
LARGE 15¾in x 13¾in (40cm x 35cm)

YARN CHOICES

Small: Patons Fairytale Dreamtime 4ply Turquoise 02935, Patons Diploma Gold 4ply Delphinium 04299

Medium: Rowan Pure Wool Aran Vert 686 and Splash 701

Large: (not shown) Rowan Big Wool or any similar weight super-bulky (chunky) yarn

T

GET KNITTING

Top bar of letter

Beginning at top of letter with letter upside down cont as folls:

Using simple sock cast on method (see Techniques), cast on 62 sts.

Rnd 1 K62.

Divide sts equally between 2 circular ndls (31 sts on each ndl), with yarn at tip of RH ndl – have LH sts at top of ndl to be worked. PM.

Rnds 2–6 K62.

Shape tip of left side

Work short rows (see Techniques) as folls:

Short row 1 K6, w+t.

Short row 2 *P12, w+t.

Short row 3 K11, w+t.

Short row 4 P10, w+t.

Short row 5 K9, w+t.

Short row 6 P8, w+t.

Short row 7 K7, w+t.

Short row 8 P6, w+t.

Short row 9 K5, w+t.

Short row 10 P4, w+t.

Short row 11 K3, w+t.

Short row 12 P2, w+t.

Short row 13 K1.**

Cut yarn leaving a tail end twice the length of sts on one ndl.

Using Kitchener stitch (see Techniques) graft together next 2 sets of 10 sts. (42 sts rem)

Central stem

With RS facing and letter upside down, rejoin yarn to rem 42 sts.

K11, sl next 10 sts onto spare dpn and set aside, sl next 10 sts (from back of right side) onto another dpn and set aside, k11. (22 sts)

Rnd 8 K22.

Rep last rnd 45 times.

Rnd 54 (inc) Kfb, k1, m1, k7, m1, k1, kfb, kfb, k1, m1, k7, m1, k1, kfb. (30 sts)

Rnd 55 K30.

Rnd 56 (inc) Kfb, k1, m1, k11, m1, k1, kfb, kfb, k1, m1, k11, m1, k1, kfb. (38 sts)

Rnd 57 K38.

Rep last rnd 3 times.

Cut yarn leaving a tail end 5 times longer than length of sts on one ndl.

Right side

Rejoin yarn to inner edge and work short rows to shape tip of right side of letter as folls:

short row 1 K16, w+t.

Work as short rows for tip of left side from * to **.

Cut yarn leaving a tail end 4 times longer than length of sts on one ndl.

TO FINISH OFF

Stuff letter firmly and evenly.

Graft together rem sts using Kitchener stitch. Weave in tail ends.

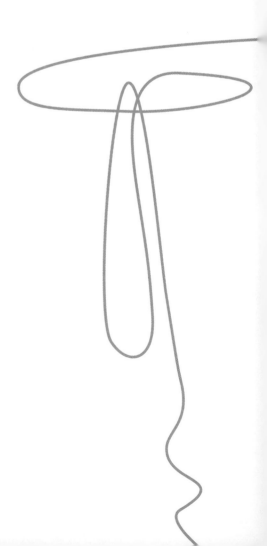

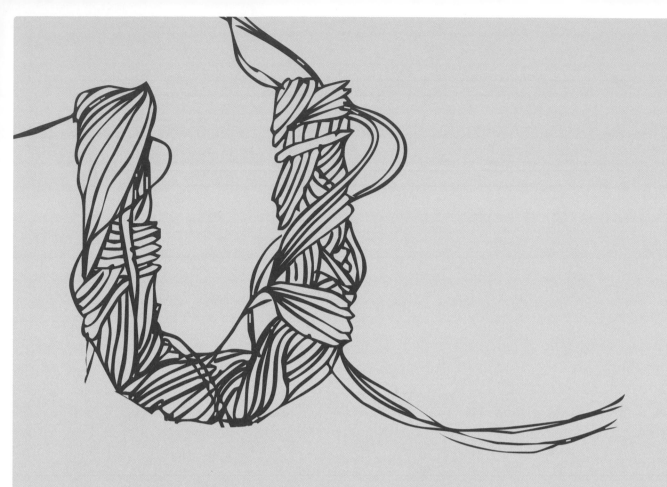

YOU WILL NEED

SMALL
18½yds (17m) of fingering-weight (4ply) yarn
1 set of 5 dpns size 1 (2.5mm)
2 sets of size 1 (2.5mm) circular needles

MEDIUM
46yds (42m) of worsted weight (Aran) yarn
1 set of 5 dpns size 8 (5mm)
2 sets of size 8 (5mm) circular needles

LARGE
118yds (108m) of super-bulky (chunky) yarn
1 set of 5 dpns size 8 (5mm)
2 sets of size 8 (5mm) circular needles

NOTIONS
Blunt-ended tapestry needle
Toy filling
Row counter

GAUGE (TENSION)
SMALL 30 sts x 39 rows to 4in (10cm) over st st
MEDIUM 18 sts x 25 rows to 4in (10cm) over st st
LARGE 7.5 sts x 10 rows to 4in (10cm) over st st

FINISHED SIZE (APPROX)
SMALL 5½in x 4¼in (14cm x 11cm)
MEDIUM 9in x 6¾in (23cm x 17cm)
LARGE 15¾in x 13¾in (40cm x 35cm)

YARN CHOICES

Small: Patons Fairytale Dreamtime 4ply Lime 02936

Medium: (not shown) Rowan Pure Wool Aran
or any similar weight worsted/aran yarn

Large: Rowan Big Wool Reseda 069

GET KNITTING

Beginning at bottom of letter, RS facing, work bottom curve as folls:

Using simple sock cast on method (see Techniques), cast on 34 sts, (17 sts on each ndl).

Rnd 1 (inc) K1, kfb, k13, kfb, k1, k1, kfb, k13, kfb, k1. (38 sts)

Divide sts equally between 2 circular ndls (19 sts on each ndl), with yarn at tip of RH ndl – have LH sts at top of ndl to be worked. PM.

Rnd 2 K38.

Rnd 3 (inc) K1, kfb, k15, kfb, k1, k1, kfb, k15, kfb, k1. (42 sts)

Rnd 4 K42.

Rnd 5 (inc) K1, kfb, k17, kfb, k1, k1, kfb, k17, kfb, k1. (46 sts)

Rnd 6 K46.

Rnd 7 (inc) K1, kfb, k19, kfb, k1, k1, kfb, k19, kfb, k1. (50 sts)

Rnd 8 K50.

Separate left side from right side

Rnd 9 K1, kfb, k2, k2tog, bind (cast) off 10 sts, k7, kfb, k1, k1, kfb, k8, bind (cast) off 11 sts, k2, kfb, k1.

Right side

Rnd 10 K6, sl next 11 sts from front of left side off circular ndl onto a dpn and set aside, sl next 11 sts from back of right side off circular and onto another dpn and set aside, k6. (12 sts for right side of letter.)

Rnd 11 K12.

Join in the rnd.

Rep last rnd 42 times.

Rnd 54 (inc) Kfb, k1, m1, k2, m1, k1, kfb, kfb, k1, m1, k2, m1, k1, kfb. (20 sts)

Rnd 55 K20.

Rnd 56 (inc) Kfb, k1, m1, k6, m1, k1, kfb, kfb, k1, m1, k6, m1, k1, kfb. (28 sts)

Rnd 57 K28.

Rep last rnd 3 times.

Cut yarn leaving a tail end 5 times the length of sts on one ndl.

Stuff this side of letter firmly.

Hold the two sets of 14 sts parallel in your left hand. Thread the cut yarn end with a sewing needle then work Kitchener stitch (see Techniques) to close the seam. Weave in tail end.

Left side

RS facing rejoin yarn to 22 sts from left side.

Rnd 10 K22.

Join in the rnd.

Rep last rnd 43 times.

Rnd 54 (inc) Kfb, k1, m1, k7, m1, k1, kfb, kfb, k1, m1, k7, m1, k1, kfb. (30 sts)

Rnd 55 K30.

Rnd 56 (inc) Kfb, k1, m1, k11, m1, k1, kfb, kfb, k1, m1, k11, m1, k1, kfb. (38 sts)

Rnd 57 K38.

Rep last rnd 3 times.

Cut yarn leaving a tail end 5 times the length of sts on one ndl.

Stuff the letter firmly and evenly.

Hold the two sets of 19 sts parallel in your left hand. Thread the cut yarn end with a sewing needle then work Kitchener stitch to close the seam neatly. Weave in tail end.

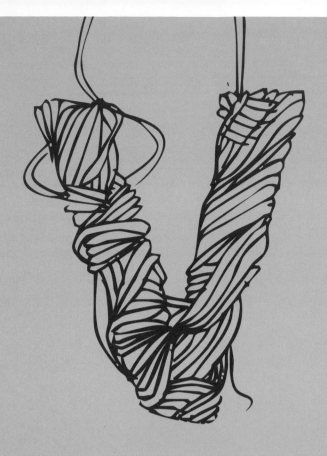

YOU WILL NEED

SMALL
35yds (32m) of fingering-weight (4ply) yarn
1 set of 5 dpns size 1 (2.5mm)
2 sets of size 1 (2.5mm) circular needles

MEDIUM
65½yds (60m) of worsted weight (Aran) yarn
1 set of 5 dpns size 8 (5mm)
2 sets of size 8 (5mm) circular needles

LARGE
109yds (100m) of super-bulky (chunky) yarn
1 set of 5 dpns size 15 (10mm)
2 sets of size 15 (10mm) circular needles

NOTIONS
Blunt-ended tapestry needle
Toy filling
Row counter

GAUGE (TENSION)
SMALL 30 sts x 39 rows to 4in (10cm) over st st
MEDIUM 18 sts x 25 rows to 4in (10cm) over st st
LARGE 7.5 sts x 10 rows to 4in (10cm) over st st

FINISHED SIZE (APPROX)
SMALL 6in x 5½in (15cm x 14cm)
MEDIUM 9in x 9½in (23cm x 24cm)
LARGE 15¾in x 13¾in (40cm x 35cm)

YARN CHOICES

Small: Rowan Pure Wool 4ply Shale 402

Medium: Rowan Creative Focus Worsted Rose 02755

Large: (not shown) Rowan Big Wool or any
similar weight super-bulky (chunky) yarn

V

GET KNITTING

Narrow side

Working from the top with letter upside down cont as folls:

Using simple sock cast on method (see Techniques), cast on 28 sts.

Rnd 1 K28.

Divide sts equally between 2 circular ndls (14 sts on each ndl), with yarn at tip of RH ndl – have LH sts at top of ndl to be worked. PM.

Rnds 2–4 K28.

Rnd 5 (dec) Skpo, k2tog, k6, skpo, k2tog, skpo, k2tog, k6, skpo, k2tog. (20 sts)

Rnd 6 K20.

Rnd 7 (dec) Skpo, k2tog, k2, skpo, k2tog, skpo, k2tog, k2, skpo, k2tog. (12 sts)

Rnd 8 K12.

Rnd 9 K1, kfb, k1, k2tog, k1, k1, skpo, k1, kfb, k1.

Rep last 2 rnds 19 times.

Cut yarn and sl two sets of sts onto 2 dpns and set aside.

Wide side

Using simple sock cast on method, cast on 38 sts.

Rnd 1 K38.

Divide sts equally between 2 circular ndls (19 sts on each ndl), with yarn at tip of RH ndl – have LH sts at top of ndl to be worked. PM.

Rnds 2–4 K38.

Rnd 5 (dec) Skpo, k2tog, k11, skpo, k2tog, skpo, k2tog, k11, skpo, k2tog. (30 sts)

Rnd 6 K30.

Rnd 7 (dec) Skpo, k2tog, k7, skpo, k2tog, skpo, k2tog, k7, skpo, k2tog. (22 sts)

Rnd 8 K22.

Rnd 9 K1, skpo, k6, kfb, k1, k1, kfb, k6, k2tog, k1.

Rep last 2 rnds 19 times.

Join sides together

Rnd 48 K11 sts from back of right side, then onto another ndl k11 from front of left side, k6 from left side onto same ndl, slide next 6 sts from back of left side to join rem 11 sts and k across onto first ndl. (34 sts – 17 sts on each ndl)

Rnd 49 (dec) K1, skpo, k11, k2tog, k1, k1, skpo, k11, k2tog, k1. (30 sts)

Rnd 50 K30.

Rnd 51 (dec) K1, skpo, k9, k2tog, k1, k1, skpo, k9, k2tog, k1. (26 sts)

Rnd 52 K26.

Rnd 53 (dec) K1, skpo, k7, k2tog, k1, k1, skpo, k7, k2tog, k1. (22 sts)

Rnd 54 K22.

Rnd 55 (dec) K1, skpo, k5, k2tog, k1, k1, skpo, k5, k2tog, k1. (18 sts)

Rnd 56 K18.

Rnd 57 (dec) K1, skpo, k3, k2tog, k1, k1, skpo, k3, k2tog, k1. (14 sts)

Rnd 58 K14.

Rnd 59 (dec) K1, skpo, k1, k2tog, k1, k1, skpo, k1, k2tog, k1. (10 sts)

Rnd 60 (dec) Skpo, k1, k2tog, skpo, k1, k2tog. (6 sts) Cut yarn, thread end through rem 6 sts, pull tight to close the gap and weave in end to secure.

TO FINISH OFF

Stuff the letter firmly and evenly through openings.

Close seams with mattress stitch. Weave in tail ends.

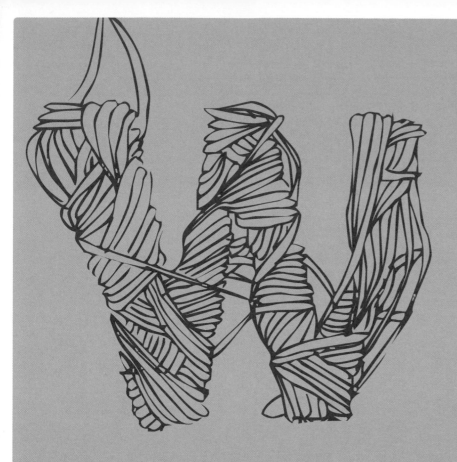

YOU WILL NEED

SMALL
70yds (64m) of fingering-weight (4ply) yarn
1 set of 5 dpns size 1 (2.5mm)
2 sets of size 1 (2.5mm) circular needles

MEDIUM
98½yds (90m) of worsted weight (Aran) yarn
1 set of 5 dpns size 8 (5mm)
2 sets of size 8 (5mm) circular needles

LARGE
120 yds (110m) of super-bulky (chunky) yarn
1 set of 5 dpns size 15 (10mm)
2 sets of size 15 (10mm) circular needles

NOTIONS
Blunt-ended tapestry needle
6 extra dpns for stitch holders
Toy filling
Row counter

GAUGE (TENSION)
SMALL 30 sts x 39 rows to 4in (10cm) over st st
MEDIUM 18sts x 22 rows to 4in(10cm) over st st
LARGE 7.5 sts x 10 rows to 4in (10cm) over st st

FINISHED SIZE (APPROX)
SMALL 5¼in x 8in (13.5cm x 20cm)
MEDIUM 10¼ x 9in (26cm x 23cm)
LARGE 15¾in x 16in (42cm x 40cm)

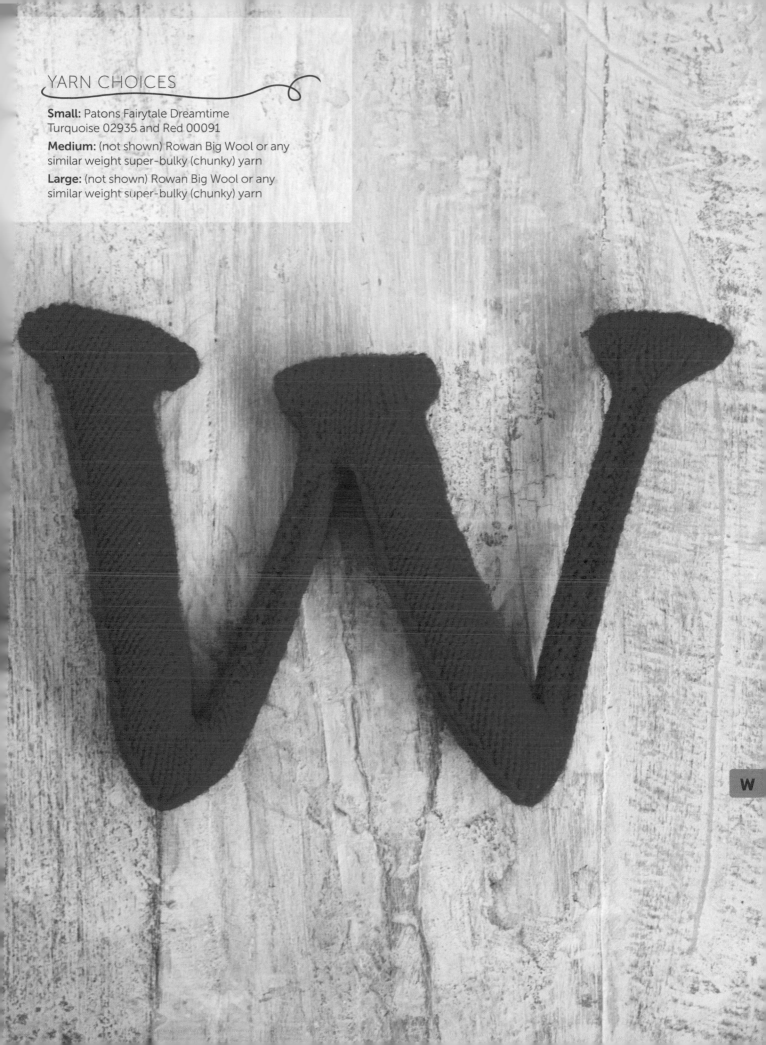

YARN CHOICES

Small: Patons Fairytale Dreamtime
Turquoise 02935 and Red 00091

Medium: (not shown) Rowan Big Wool or any
similar weight super-bulky (chunky) yarn

Large: (not shown) Rowan Big Wool or any
similar weight super-bulky (chunky) yarn

W

GET KNITTING

First leg

Working from top of letter with W upside down work the first leg, wide slant as folls:

*Cast on 38 sts using simple sock cast on method (see Techniques).

Rnd 1 K38.

Divide sts equally between 2 circular ndls (19 sts on each ndl), with yarn at tip of RH ndl – have LH sts at top of ndl to be worked. PM.

Rnds 2–4 K38.

Rnd 5 (dec) Skpo, k2tog, k11, skpo, k2tog, skpo, k2tog, k11, skpo, k2tog. (30 sts)

Rnd 6 K30.

Rnd 7 (dec) Skpo, k2tog, k7, skpo, k2tog, skpo, k2tog, k7, skpo, k2tog. (22 sts)

Rnd 8 K22.

Rnd 9 K1, skpo, k6, kfb, k1, k1, kfb, k6, k2tog k1.**

Rep last 2 rnds 19 times ending with front of letter facing ready to be worked.

Cut yarn. Leave sts on spare dpns and set aside.

Fourth leg

Work the fourth leg, the narrowest and furthest right, as folls:

Cast on 28 sts using simple sock cast on method.

Rnd 1 K28.

Divide sts equally between 2 circular ndls (14 sts on each ndl), with yarn at tip of RH ndl – have LH sts at top of ndl to be worked. PM.

Rnds 2–4 K28.

Rnd 5 (dec) Skpo, k2tog, k6, skpo, k2tog, skpo, k2tog, k6, skpo, k2tog. (20 sts)

Rnd 6 K20.

Rnd 7 (dec) Skpo, k2tog, k2, skpo, k2tog, skpo, k2tog, k2, skpo, k2tog.** (12 sts)

Rnd 8 K12.

Rnd 9 K1, kfb, k1, k2tog, k1, k1, skpo, k1, kfb, k1.

Rep last 2 rnds 19 times ending with front of letter facing ready to be worked.

Cut yarn. Leave sts on spare dpns and set aside.

Third leg

Work the third leg, wide slant, as for first leg from * to **.

Following on from third leg above cont as folls:

Add second leg

Rnd 10 K1, kfb, k7, kfb, k1, k1, kfb, k7, kfb, k1. (26 sts)

Rnd 11 K26.

Rnd 12 K1, kfb, k9, kfb, k1, k1, kfb, k9, kfb, k1. (30 sts)

Rnd 13 K30.

Rnd 14 K1, kfb, k11, kfb, k1, k1, kfb, k11, kfb, k1. (34 sts)

Separate second leg from third leg

Rnd 15 K6, sl next 11 sts onto spare dpn and set aside, sl next 11 sts onto separate dpn and set aside, k rem 6 sts. (12 sts)

Rnd 16 K1, kfb, k1, k2tog, k1, k1, skpo, k1, kfb, k1.

Rnd 17 K12.

Rep last 2 rnds 15 times ending with front of letter facing ready to knit.

Cut yarn. Leave sts on spare dpns and set aside.

Join second and first legs at apex

Rnd 48 With RS facing, onto circular ndl, join first 11 sts held on dpns from first leg, rejoin yarn, k these 11 sts, k6 from front of second leg onto same ndl (the angles of the legs should be facing in towards each other). Onto another circular ndl, sl 6 sts from back of second leg and k across them, k11 from back of first leg. (34 sts – 17 sts on each ndl)

Rnd 49 (dec) K1, skpo, k11, k2tog, k1, k1, skpo, k11, k2tog, k1. (30 sts)

Rnd 50 K30.

Rnd 51 (dec) K1, skpo, k9, k2tog, k1, k1, skpo, k9, k2tog, k1. (26 sts)

Rnd 52 K26.

Rnd 53 (dec) K1, skpo, k7, k2tog, k1, k1, skpo, k7, k2tog, k1. (22 sts)

Rnd 54 K22.

Rnd 55 (dec) K1, skpo, k5, k2tog, k1, k1, skpo, k5, k2tog, k1. (18 sts)

Rnd 56 K18.

Rnd 57 (dec) K1, skpo, k3, k2tog, k1, k1, skpo, k3, k2tog, k1. (14 sts)

Rnd 58 K14.

Rnd 59 (dec) K1, skpo, k1, k2tog, k1, k1, skpo, k1, k2tog, k1. (10 sts)

Rnd 60 (dec) Skpo, k1, k2tog, skpo, k1, k2tog. (6 sts)

Cut yarn, thread end through rem 6 sts, pull up tight to close the gap and weave in the end to secure.

Complete third leg

With RS facing, sl 11 sts from front of third leg onto a circular ndl, sl 11 sts from back of third leg on another circular ndl. (22 sts)

Join in the rnd.

Rnd 16 K1, skpo, k6, kfb, k1, k1, kfb, k6, k2tog, k1.

Rnd 17 K22.

Rep last 2 rnds 15 times.

Rnd 48 K1, skpo, k6, kfb, k1, k1, kfb, k6, k2tog, k1.

Join third and fourth legs at apex

K11, then k6 from front of fourth leg onto same ndl – the angles of the legs should be facing in towards each other. Onto another circular ndl sl 6 sts from back of fourth leg and k these sts, then k11 from back of third leg. (34 sts – 17 on each ndl)

Rnd 49 (dec) K1, skpo, k11, k2tog, k1, k1, skpo, k11, k2tog, k1. (30 sts)

Rnd 50 K30.

Rnd 51 (dec) K1, skpo, k9, k2tog, k1, k1, skpo, k9, k2tog, k1. (26 sts)

Rnd 52 K26.

Rnd 53 (dec) K1, skpo, k7, k2tog, k1, k1, skpo, k7, k2tog, k1. (22 sts)

Rnd 54 K22.

Rnd 55 (dec) K1, skpo, k5, k2tog, k1, k1, skpo, k5, k2tog, k1. (18 sts)

Rnd 56 K18.

Stuff letter firmly and evenly before completing as follows:

Rnd 57 (dec) K1, skpo, k3, k2tog, k1, k1, skpo, k3, k2tog, k1. (14 sts)

Rnd 58 K14.

Rnd 59 (dec) K1, skpo, k1, k2tog, k1, k1, skpo, k1, k2tog, k1. (10 sts)

Rnd 60 (dec) Skpo, k1, k2tog, skpo, k1, k2tog. (6 sts)

TO FINISH OFF

Cut yarn, thread end through the rem 6 sts, pull up tight to close the gap and weave in the end to secure.

W

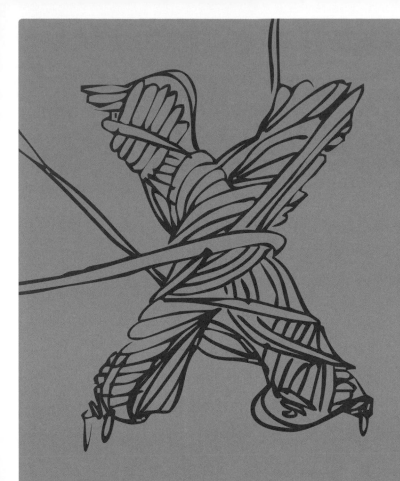

YOU WILL NEED

SMALL
33 yds (30m) of fingering-weight (4ply) yarn
1 set of 5 dpns size 1 (2.5mm)
2 sets of size 1 (2.5mm) circular needles

MEDIUM
104yds (95m) of worsted weight (Aran) yarn
1 set of 5 dpns size 8 (5mm)
2 sets of size 8 (5mm) circular needles

LARGE
120yds (110m) of super-bulky (chunky) yarn
1 set of 5 dpns size 15 (10mm)
2 sets of size 15 (10mm) circular needles

NOTIONS
Blunt-ended tapestry needle
Toy filling
Row counter
2 extra dpns for stitch holders

GAUGE (TENSION)
SMALL 30 sts x 39 rows to 4in (10cm) over st st
MEDIUM 18 sts x 25 rows to 4in (10cm) over st st
LARGE 7.5 sts x 10 rows to 4in (10mm) over st st

FINISHED SIZE (APPROX)
SMALL 5¼in x 4¼in (13.5cm x 11cm)
MEDIUM 9in x 8in (23cm x 20cm)
LARGE 15¾in x 13¾in (40cm x 35cm)

YARN CHOICES

Small: Patons Fairytale Dreamtime
4ply Hot Pink 02939

Medium: Rowan Pure Wool Aran Burnt 700, Rowan
Creative Focus Worsted Deep Rose 02755

Large: (not shown) Rowan Big Wool or any
similar weight super-bulky (chunky) yarn

X

GET KNITTING

First leg top left

With RS facing using simple sock cast on method (see Techniques), cast on 38 sts.

Rnd 1 K38.

Divide sts equally between 2 circular ndls (19 sts on each ndl), with yarn at tip of RH ndl – have LH sts at top of ndl to be worked. PM.

Rnds 2-4 K38.

Rnd 5 (dec) Skpo, k2tog, k11, skpo, k2tog, skpo, k2tog, k11, skpo, k2tog. (30 sts)

Rnd 6 K30.

Rnd 7 (dec) Skpo, k2tog, k7, skpo, k2tog, skpo, k2tog, k7, skpo, k2tog. (22 sts)

Rnd 8 K22.

Rnd 9 K1, kfb, k6, k2tog, k1, k1, skpo, k6, kfb, k1.

Rep last 2 rnds 7 times ending at left back.

Cut yarn and sl two sets of sts onto 2 dpns and set aside.

Second leg top right

Using simple sock cast on method, cast on 28 sts.

Rnd 1 K28.

Divide sts equally between 2 circular ndls (14 sts on each ndl), with yarn at tip of RH ndl – have LH sts at top of ndl to be worked. PM.

Rnds 2–4 K28.

Rnd 5 (dec) Skpo, k2tog, k6, skpo, k2tog, skpo, k2tog, k6, skpo, k2tog. (20 sts)

Rnd 6 K20.

Rnd 7 (dec) Skpo, k2tog, k2, skpo, k2tog, skpo, k2tog, k2, skpo, k2tog. (12 sts)

Rnd 8 K12.

Rnd 9 K1, skpo, k1, kfb, k1, k1, kfb, k1, k2tog, k1.

Rep last 2 rnds 7 times.

Join at centre of X

Rnd 24 K6 from circular needle, k11 from left front onto same ndl, sl next 11 sts from front of left side onto another circular ndl, k11 then k6 from front of right side. (34 sts – 17 sts on each ndl) Join in the rnd.

Rnd 25 (dec) K1, skpo, k11, k2tog, k1, k1, skpo, k11, k2tog, k1. (30 sts)

Rnd 26 K30.

Rnd 27 (dec) K1, skpo, k9, k2tog, k1, k1, skpo, k9, k2tog, k1. (26 sts)

Rnd 28 K26.

Rnd 29 (dec) K1, skpo, k7, k2tog, k1, k1, skpo, k7, k2tog, k1. (22 sts)

Rnd 30 K22.

Rnd 31 (inc) K1, kfb, k7, kfb, k1, k1, kfb, k7, kfb, k1. (26 sts)

Rnd 32 K26.

Rnd 33 (inc) k1, kfb, k9, kfb, k1, k1, kfb, k9, kfb, k1. (30 sts)

Rnd 34 K30.

Rnd 35 (inc) k1, kfb, k11, kfb, k1, k1, kfb, k11, kfb, k1. (34 sts)

Separate the two legs

Rnd 36 K11, sl next 6 sts off ndl onto spare dpn, sl next 6 sts onto another dpn, k11 onto second circular ndl. Set aside dpns and cont on circular ndls only. Join in the rnd.

Rnd 37 K1, kfb, k6, k2tog, k1, k1, skpo, k6, kfb, k1.

Rnd 38 K22.

Rep last 2 rnds 7 times.

Rnd 53 (inc) Kfb, k1, m1, k7, m1, k1, kfb, kfb, k1, m1, k7, m1, k1, kfb. (30 sts)

Rnd 54 K30.

Rnd 55 (inc) Kfb, k1, m1, k11, m1, k1, kfb, kfb, k1, m1, k11, m1, k1, kfb. (38 sts)

Rnd 56 K38.

Rep last rnd 3 times.

Cut yarn leaving 12in (30cm) tail end.

Sew up leg

Hold two sets of 19 sts parallel in your left hand. Thread cut yarn end with a sewing needle then work Kitchener stitch (see Techniques) to close the seam. Weave in tail end.

Bottom left leg

Rejoin yarn to rem 12 sts at inner edge. Working with dpns or spare circulars cont as folls:

Rnd 36 K12. Join in the rnd.

Rnd 37 K1, skpo, k1, kfb, k1, k1, kfb, k1, k2tog, k1.

Rnd 38 K12.

Rep last 2 rnds 7 times.

Rnd 53 (inc) Kfb, k1, m1, k2, m1, k1,

kfb, kfb, k1, m1, k2, m1, k1, kfb. (20 sts)

Rnd 54 K20.

Rnd 55 (inc) Kfb, k1, m1, k6, m1, k1, kfb, kfb, k1, m1, k6, m1, k1, kfb. (28 sts)

Rnd 56 K28.

Rep last rnd 3 times.

Cut yarn, leaving a tail end 5 times the length of sts on one ndl.

TO FINISH OFF

Stuff letter firmly and evenly.

Hold 2 sets of 14 sts parallel in your left hand. Thread cut yarn end with a sewing needle then work Kitchener stitch to close the seam neatly. Weave in tail ends.

X

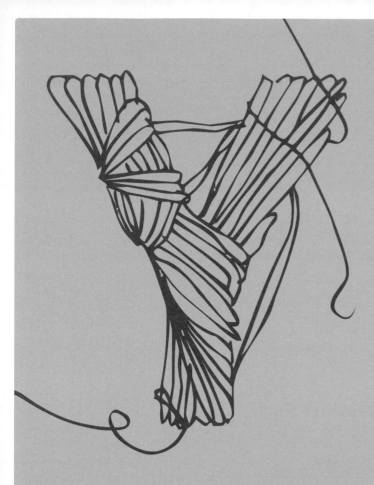

YOU WILL NEED

SMALL
35yds (32m) of fingering-weight (4ply) yarn
1 set of 5 dpns size 1 (2.5mm)
2 sets of size 1 (2.5mm) circular needles

MEDIUM
74½yds (68m) of worsted weight (Aran) yarn
1 set of 5 dpns size 8 (5mm)
2 sets of size 8 (5mm) circular needles

LARGE
109yds (100m) of super-bulky (chunky) yarn
1 set of 5 dpns size 15 (10mm)
2 sets of size 15 (10mm) circular needles

NOTIONS
Blunt-ended tapestry needle
Toy filling
Row counter

GAUGE (TENSION)
SMALL 30 sts x 39 rows to 4in (10cm) over st st
MEDIUM 18 sts x 25 rows to 4in (10cm) over st st
LARGE 7.5 sts x 10 rows to 4in (10mm) over st st

FINISHED SIZE (APPROX)
SMALL 4in x 2½in (10.5cm x 6.5cm)
MEDIUM 9in x 6¾in (23cm x 17cm)
LARGE 15¾in x 13¾in (40cm x 35cm)

Y

GET KNITTING

Left side

Beginning at top of letter with letter upside down and with WS facing cont as folls:

Using simple sock cast on method (see Techniques), cast on 28 sts.

Rnd 1 K28.

Divide sts equally between 2 circular ndls (14 sts on each ndl), with yarn at tip of RH ndl – have LH sts at top of ndl to be worked. PM.

Rnds 2–4 K28.

Rnd 5 (dec) Skpo, k2tog, k6, skpo, k2tog, skpo, k2tog, k6, skpo, k2tog. (20 sts)

Rnd 6 K20.

Rnd 7 (dec) Skpo, k2tog, k2, skpo, k2tog, skpo, k2tog, k2, skpo, k2tog. (12 sts)

Rnd 8 K12.

Rnd 9 K1, kfb, k1, k2tog, k1, k1, skpo, k1, kfb, k1.

Rep last 2 rnds 7 times ending at back of right side of letter.

Cut yarn and sl two sets of sts onto 2 dpns and set aside.

Right side

Using simple sock cast on method, cast on 38 sts.

Rnd 1 K38.

Divide sts equally between 2 circular ndls (19 sts on each ndl), with yarn at tip of RH ndl – have LH sts at top of ndl to be worked. PM.

Rnds 2–4 K38.

Rnd 5 (dec) Skpo, k2tog, k11, skpo, k2tog, skpo, k2tog, k11, skpo, k2tog. (30 sts)

Rnd 6 K30.

Rnd 7 (dec) Skpo, k2tog, k7, skpo, k2tog, skpo, k2tog, k7, skpo, k2tog. (22 sts)

Rnd 8 K22.

Rnd 9 K1, skpo, k6, kfb, k1, k1, kfb, k6, k2tog, k1.

Rep last 2 rnds 7 times.

Join both sides

Rnd 24 K11 from front left side, onto same ndl k6 from front right side, sl next 6 sts from back of right side onto another circular ndl, k11 from back of left side. (34 sts – 17 sts on each ndl) Join in the rnd.

Rnd 25 (dec) K1, skpo, k11, k2tog, k1, k1, skpo, k11, k2tog, k1. (30 sts)

Rnd 26 K30.

Rnd 27 (dec) K1, skpo, k9, k2tog, k1, k1, skpo, k9, k2tog, k1. (26 sts)

Rnd 28 K26.

Rnd 29 (dec) K1, skpo, k7, k2tog, k1, k1, skpo, k7, k2tog, k1. (22 sts)

Rnd 30 K22.

Rep last rnd 23 times.

Rnd 54 (inc) Kfb, k1, m1, k7, m1, k1, kfb, kfb, k1, m1, k7, m1, k1, kfb. (30 sts)

Rnd 55 K30.

Rnd 56 (inc) Kfb, k1, m1, k11, m1, k1, kfb, kfb, k1, m1, k11, m1, k1, kfb. (38 sts)

Rnd 57 K38.

Rep last rnd 3 times.

Cut yarn leaving a tail end 5 times longer than length of sts on one ndl.

TO FINISH OFF

Stuff letter firmly and evenly.

Hold 2 sets of 19 sts parallel in your left hand. Thread cut yarn end with a sewing needle then work Kitchener stitch (see Techniques) to close the seam neatly. Weave in tail ends.

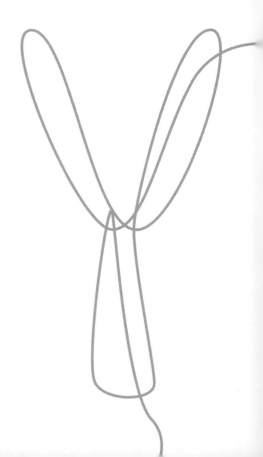

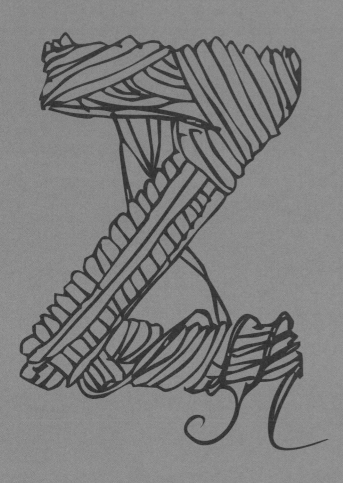

YOU WILL NEED

SMALL
19¾yds (18m) of fingering-weight (4ply) yarn
1 set of 5 dpns size 1 (2.5mm)
2 sets of size 1 (2.5mm) circular needles

MEDIUM
98½yds (90m) of worsted weight (Aran) yarn
1 set of 5 dpns size 8 (5mm)
2 sets of size 8 (5mm) circular needles

LARGE
109½yds (100m) of super-bulky (chunky) yarn
1 set of 5 dpns size 15 (10mm)
2 sets of size 15 (10mm) circular needles

NOTIONS
Blunt-ended tapestry needle
2 extra dpns for stitch holders
Toy filling
Row counter

GAUGE (TENSION)

SMALL 30 sts x 39 rows to 4in (10cm) over st st

MEDIUM 18 sts x 25 rows to 4in (10cm) over st st

LARGE 7.5 sts x 10 rows to 4in (10cm) over st st

FINISHED SIZE (APPROX)

SMALL 5¼in x 4¼in (13.5cm x 11cm)

MEDIUM 10¼in x 7½in (26cm x 19cm)

LARGE 15¾in x 13½in (40cm x 34cm)

YARN CHOICES

Small: Patons Fairytale Dreamtime 4ply Red 00091

Medium: (not shown) Rowan Pure Wool Aran or any similar weight worsted/aran yarn

Large: Rowan Big Wool Ice Blue 021, Reseda 069 and Steel 052

Z

GET KNITTING

Beginning at the bottom of letter with RS facing, work as folls:

Using simple sock cast on method (see Techniques), cast on 64 sts, (32 sts on each ndl).

Rnd 1 K64

Divide sts equally between 2 circular ndls (32 sts on each ndl), with yarn at tip of RH ndl – have LH sts at top of ndl to be worked. PM.

Rnds 2–7 K64.

Shape serif at right side

Work short rows (see Techniques) as folls:

Short row 1 *K6, w+t.

Short row 2 P12, w+t.

Short row 3 K11, w+t.

Short row 4 P10, w+t.

Short row 5 K9, w+t.

Short row 6 P8, w+t.

Short row 7 K7, w+t.

Short row 8 P6, w+t.

Short row 9 K5, w+t.

Short row 10 P4, w+t.

Short row 11 K3, w+t.

Short row 12 P2, w+t.

Short row 13 K1.*

Cut yarn leaving a tail end twice the length of sts on one ndl.

Using Kitchener stitch (see Techniques) graft together the next 2 sets of 21 sts (42 sts in total) so leaving 2 sets of 11 sts on ndls.

With RS of letter facing, rejoin yarn to rem 22 sts.

Join in the rnd.

Create slant

Rnd 8 K1, kfb, k6, k2tog, k1, k1, skpo, k6, kfb, k1. PM.

Rnd 9 K22.

Rep last 2 rnds 22 times.

Rnd 53 K1, kfb, k6, k2tog, k1, k1, skpo, k6, kfb, k1. Remove marker.

Increase for top of letter

Next rnd (inc) K11, with WS facing cast on 19 sts, p41, with RS facing cast on 19 sts. (60 sts)

Work short rows for serif as before from * to * joining back into the rnd as you do so.

Next rnd (inc) K28, kfb, k1, k1, kfb, k28. (62 sts)

Next rnd K62.

Next rnd (inc) K29, kfb, k1, k1, kfb, k29. (64 sts)

Next rnd K64.

Rep last rnd 3 times.

Cut yarn leaving a tail end 5 times the length of sts on one ndl.

Hold two sets of 32 sts parallel in your left hand. Thread the cut yarn end with a sewing needle then work Kitchener stitch to close the seam neatly. Weave in the tail end.

TO FINISH OFF

Stuff letter firmly and evenly. Close the opening with mattress stitch.

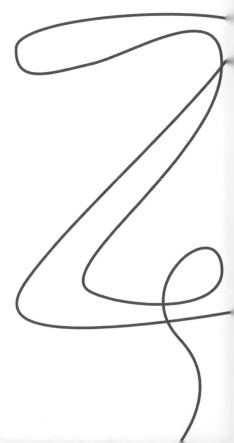

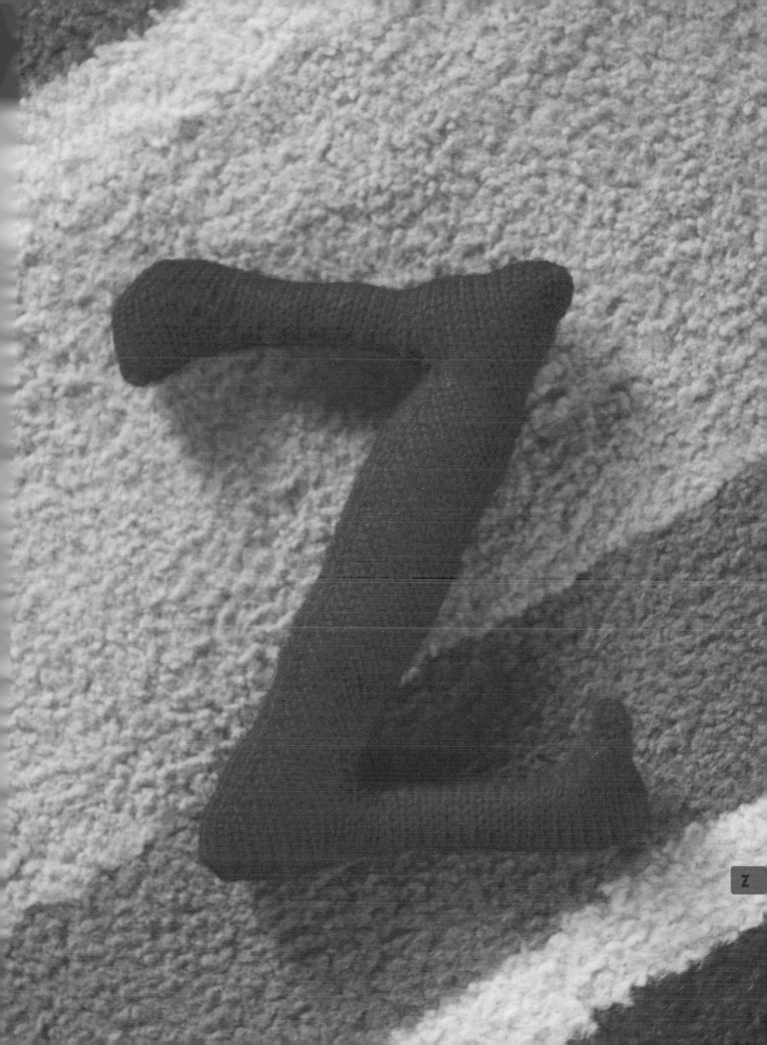

YARN CHOICES

Small: Patons Fairytale Dreamtime 4ply Hot Pink 02939, Red 00091, Turquoise 02935, Patons Diploma Gold 4ply New Berry 04294, Delphinium 04299, Patons Fairytale Soft 4ply Baby Blue 4310

Medium/Large: (not shown) Rowan Pure Wool Aran or any similar weight worsted/aran yarn

YOU WILL NEED

SMALL
53½yds (49m) of fingering-weight (4ply) yarn
1 set of 5 dpns size 1 (2.5mm)
2 sets of size 1 (2.5mm) circular needles

MEDIUM
104yds (95m) of worsted weight (Aran) yarn
1 set of 5 dpns size 8 (5mm)
2 sets of size 8 (5mm) circular needles

LARGE
120yds (110m) of super-bulky (chunky) yarn
1 set of 5 dpns size 15 (10mm)
2 sets of size 15 (10mm) circular needles

NOTIONS
Blunt-ended tapestry needle
2 extra dpns for stitch holders
Toy filling
Row counter

GAUGE (TENSION)

SMALL 30 sts x 39 rows to 4in (10cm) over st st
MEDIUM 18 sts x 25 rows to 4in (10cm) over st st
LARGE 7.5 sts x 10 rows to 4in (10cm) over st st

FINISHED SIZE (APPROX)

SMALL 5¼in x 4¼in (13.5cm x 11cm)
MEDIUM 9in x 8¾in (23cm x 22cm)
LARGE 15¾in x 13¾in (40cm x 35cm)

&: GET KNITTING

Far right of letter

Beg with narrow sweep at far right of letter cont as folls:

Using simple sock cast on method (see Techniques), cast on 28 sts.

Rnd 1 K28.

Divide sts equally between 2 circular ndls (14 sts on each ndl), with yarn at tip of RH ndl – have LH sts at top of ndl to be worked. PM.

Rnds 2–4 K28.

Rnd 5 (dec) Skpo, k2tog, k6, skpo, k2tog, skpo, k2tog, k6, skpo, k2tog. (20 sts)

Rnd 6 K20.

Rnd 7 (dec) Skpo, k2tog, k2, skpo, k2tog, skpo, k2tog, k2, skpo, k2tog. (12 sts)

Rnd 8 K12.

Rnd 9 K1, skpo, k1, kfb, k1, k1, kfb, k1, k2tog, k1.

Rnds 10–13 K12.

Rnds 14–43 Rep last 5 rnds 6 more times.

Increase for left-hand curve

Rnd 44 (inc) K1, kfb, k4, k4, kfb, k1. (14 sts)

Rnd 45 (inc) K5, kfb, k1, k1, kfb, k5. (16 sts)

Rnd 46 (inc) K1, kfb, k6, k6, kfb, k1. (18 sts)

Rnd 47 (inc) K7, kfb, k1, k1, kfb, k7. (20 sts)

Rnd 48 (inc) K1, kfb, k8, k8, kfb, k1. (22 sts)

Rnd 49 (inc) K9, kfb, k1, k1, kfb, k9. (24 sts)

Shape right curve

Work short rows (see Techniques) to complete the right curve as folls:

Short row 1 K11, w+t.

Short row 2 P22, w+t.

Short row 3 K21, w+t.

Short row 4 P20, w+t.

Short row 5 K19, w+t.

Short row 6 P18, w+t.

Short row 7 K17, w+t.

Short row 8 P16, w+t.

Short row 9 K15, w+t.

Short row 10 P14, w+t

Short row 11 K13, w+t.

Short row 12 P12, w+t.

Short row 13 K11, w+t.

Short row 14 P10, w+t.

Short row 15 K9, w+t.

Short row 16 P8, w+t.

Short row 17 K7, w+t.

Short row 18 P6, w+t.

Short row 19 K5, w+t.

Short row 20 P4, w+t.

Short row 21 K3, w+t.

Short row 22 P2, w+t.

Short row 23 K1.

Join back into rnd.

Rnd 50 K24.

Rnd 51 (dec) K1, skpo, k9, k9, k2tog, k1. (22 sts)

Rnd 52 (dec) K8, k2tog, k1, k1, skpo, k8. (20 sts)

Rnd 53 (dec) K1, skpo, k7, k7, k2tog, k1. (18 sts)

Rnd 54 (dec) K6, k2tog, k1, k1, skpo, k6. (16 sts)

Rnd 55 (dec) K1, skpo, k5, k5, k2tog, k1. (14 sts)

Rnd 56 (dec) K4, k2tog, k1, k1, skpo, k4. (12 sts)

Rnd 57–60 K12.

Rnd 61 K1, skpo, k1, kfb, k1, k1, kfb, k1, k2tog, k1.

Rep last 5 rnds 5 more times.

Rnds 87-89 K12.

Rep last rnd twice.

Rnd 90 (inc) K1, kfb, k4, k4, kfb, k1. (14 sts)

Rnd 91 (inc) K5, kfb, k1, k1, kfb, k5. (16 sts)

Rnd 92 K16.

Shape top right curve

Work short rows to complete the right curve as folls:

Short row 1 *K15, w+t.

Short row 2 P14, w+t.

Short row 3 K13, w+t.

Short row 4 ****P12, w+t.

Short row 5 K11, w+t.

Short row 6 P10, w+t.

Short row 7 K9, w+t.

Short row 8 P8, w+t.

Short row 9 K7, w+t.

Short row 10 P6, w+t.

Short row 11 K5, w+t.

Short row 12 P4, w+t.

Short row 13 K3, w+t.

Short row 14 P2, w+t.

Short row 15 K9.

Join back into the rnd.

Rnd 93 K16.

Rep last rnd once **.

Second curve

Work short rows to complete second curve as for top right curve from * to **:

Rnd 97 K1, skpo, k5, k5, k2tog, k1. (14 sts)

Third curve

Short row 1 K13, w + t.

Work short rows to complete third curve as for top right curve from short row 4 to **:

Rnd 100 (inc) K5, kfb, k1, k1, kfb, k5. (16 sts)

Rnd 101 K16.

Rnd 102 (inc) K1, kfb, k6, k6, kfb, k1. (18 sts)

Rnd 103 K7, Kfb, k1, k1, kfb, k7. (20 sts)

Rnd 104 K20.

Rnd 105 (inc) k1, kfb, k8, k8, kfb, k1. (22 sts)

Rnd 106 K22.

Rep last rnd once.

Stuff the knitting up to the first right side curve.

Create first channel

Rnd 108 *K11, turn, now work backwards and forwards to create the first channel:

Channel row 1 Purl.

Channel row 2 Knit.

Rep last 2 channel rows 3 times.

Channel row 9 Purl. Cut yarn.

With RS facing rejoin yarn to 11 sts on other side of channel, k across these 11 sts.

Channel row 1 Purl.

Channel row 2 Knit.

Rep last 2 channel rows twice.

Channel row 7 Purl.

Don't cut yarn. Stuff piece to here.

Slip channel over the section of stuffed knitting directly after the first short row shaping curve, then work back into the round to close the channel over the stuffed knitted section:

Rnd 109 K22.**

Rep last rnd 16 times.

Create second channel

Work as first channel from * to **.

Rep last rnd twice.

Create bottom flick

Rnd 127 K1, skpo, k6, Kfb, k1, k1, Kfb, k6, k2tog, k1.

Rnd 128 K22.

Rnd 129 (dec) Skpo, k2tog, k5, kfb, k1, k1, kfb, k5, skpo, k2tog. (20 sts)

Rnd 130 K20.

Rnd 131 K1, kfb, k5, k2tog, k1, k1, skpo, k5, kfb, k1.

Rnd 132 K20.

Rep last 2 rnds 3 times.

Cut yarn leaving a tail 4 times length of sts on one dpn.

TO FINISH OFF

Stuff last section then join tog with Kitchener stitch (see Techniques).

YARN CHOICES

Small: Patons Fairytale Dreamtime 4ply Hot Pink 02939

Medium: Rowan Creative Focus Worsted shades Natural 00100 and Deep Rose 02755

Large: (not shown) Rowan Big Wool or any similar weight super-bulky (chunky) yarn

YOU WILL NEED

SMALL
50½yds (46m) of fingering-weight (4ply) yarn

1 set of 5 dpns size 1 (2.5mm)

2 sets of size 1 (2.5mm) circular needles

MEDIUM
104yds (95m) of worsted weight (Aran) yarn

1 set of 5 dpns size 8 (5mm)

2 sets of size 8 (5mm) circular needles

LARGE
120yds (110m) of super-bulky (chunky) yarn

1 set of 5 dpns size 15 (10mm)

2 sets of 5 dpns size 15 (10mm)

NOTIONS
Blunt-ended tapestry needle

2 extra dpns for stitch holders

Toy filling

Row counter

GAUGE (TENSION)

SMALL 30 sts x 39 rows to 4in (10cm) over st st

MEDIUM 18 sts x 25 rows to 4in (10cm) over st st

LARGE 7.5 sts x 10 rows to 4in (10cm) over st st

FINISHED SIZE (APPROX)

SMALL 5¼in x 4¼in (13.5cm x 11cm)

MEDIUM 8¾in x 7in (22cm x 18cm)

LARGE 15¾in x 13¾in (40cm x 35 cm)

HEART: GET KNITTING

Beg with point at bottom of heart cont as folls:

Using simple sock cast on method (see Techniques), cast on 4 sts.

Rnd 1 Kfb 4 times. (8 sts)

Divide sts equally between 2 circular ndls (4 sts on each ndl), with yarn at tip of RH ndl – have LH sts at top of ndl to be worked. PM.

Rnd 2 K8.

Rnd 3 (inc) K1, kfb, kfb, k1, k1, kfb, kfb, k1. (12 sts)

Rnd 4 K12.

Rnd 5 (inc) K1, kfb, k2, kfb, k1, k1, kfb, k2, kfb, k1. (16 sts)

Rnd 6 K16.

Rnd 7 (inc) K1, kfb, k4, kfb, k1, k1, kfb, k4, kfb, k1. (20 sts)

Rnd 8 K20.

Rnd 9 (inc) K1, kfb, k6, kfb, k1, k1, kfb, k6, kfb, k1. (24 sts)

Rnd 10 K24.

Rnd 11 (inc) K1, kfb, k8, kfb, k1, k1, kfb, k8, kfb, k1. (28 sts)

Rnd 12 K28.

Rnd 13 (inc) K1, kfb, k10, kfb, k1, k1, kfb, k10, kfb, k1. (32 sts)

Rnd 14 K32.

Rnd 15 (inc) K1, kfb, k12, kfb, k1, k1, kfb, k12, kfb, k1. (36 sts)

Rnd 16 K36.

Rnd 17 (inc) K1, kfb, k14, kfb, k1, k1, kfb, k14, kfb, k1. (40 sts)

Rnd 18 K40.

Rnd 19 (inc) K1, kfb, k16, kfb, k1, k1, kfb, k16, kfb, k1. (44 sts)

Rnd 20 K44.

Divide the right side from left

Rnd 21 K1, kfb, k6, k2tog, k1, sl next 11 sts onto a spare dpn and set aside, sl next 11 sts (from back of left side) onto another spare dpn and set aside, k1, skpo, k6, kfb, k1.

Right side

Working on 22 sts for right side only cont as folls:

Rnd 22 K22.

Rnd 23 K1, kfb, k6, k2tog, k1, k1, skpo, k6, kfb, k1.

Rep last 2 rnds 3 times.

Rnds 30–32 K22.

Rnd 33 K1, skpo, k6, kfb, k1, k1, kfb, k6, k2tog, k1.

Rnds 34 & 35 K22.

Rnds 36–47 Rep last 3 rnds 4 more times.

Rnd 48 K1, skpo, k6, kfb, k1, k1, kfb, k6, k2tog, k1.

Rnd 49 K22.

Rep last 2 rnds once.

Shape right curve

Work short rows (see Techniques) to complete the right curve as folls:

Short row 1 K10, w+t.

Short row 2 *P20, w+t.

Short row 3 K19, w+t.

Short row 4 P18, w+t.

Short row 5 K17, w+t.

Short row 6 P16, w+t.

Short row 7 K15, w+t.

Short row 8 P14, w+t.

Short row 9 K13, w+t.

Short row 10 P12, w+t.

Short row 11 K11, w+t.

Short row 12 P10, w+t.

Short row 13 K9, w+t.

Short row 14 P8, w+t.

Short row 15 K7, w+t.

Short row 16 P6, w+t.

Short row 17 K5, w+t.

Short row 18 P4, w+t.

Short row 19 K3, w+t.

Short row 20 P2, w+t.**

Short row 21 K1.

Join back into rnd.

Rnds 52 & 53 K22.

Rnd 54 K1, skpo, k6, kfb, k1, k1, kfb, k6, k2tog, k1.

Rnd 55 K22.

Rep last 2 rnds 4 more times.

Cut yarn leaving tail 9 times length of sts on one needle. Sl two sets of sts onto 2 spare dpns, set aside.

Left side

With RS facing rejoin yarn to inner edge of left side of heart.

Rnd 21 K1, skpo, k6, kfb, k1, k1, kfb, k6, k2tog, k1.

Rnd 22 K22.

Rnd 23 K1, skpo, k6, kfb, k1, k1, kfb, k6, k2tog, k1.

Rep last 2 rnds 3 times.

Rnds 30—32 K22.

Rnd 33 K1, Kfb, k6, k2tog, k1, k1, skpo, k6, kfb, k1.

Rnds 34 & 35 K22.

Rnds 36—47 Rep last 3 rnds 4 times.

Rnd 48 K1, kfb, k6, k2tog, k1, k1, skpo, k6, kfb, k1.

Rnds 49—51 K22.

Shape left curve

Work short rows to complete left curve as folls:

Short row 1 K21, w+t.

Work as Right Curve from * to **.

Short row 22 K12.

Join back into rnd.

Rnds 52 & 53 K22.

Rnd 54 K1, kfb, k6, k2tog, k1, k1, skpo, k6, kfb, k1.

Rnd 55 K22.

Rep last 2 rnds 4 times.

Cut yarn leaving a tail 9 times length of sts on one dpn.

TO FINISH OFF

Graft the front 11 sts of left side with front 11 sts of right side by threading up the length of yarn. Hold the two sets of 11 sts parallel in your left hand, securing the threaded yarn and working Kitchener stitch (see Techniques) join first side. Stuff the shape firmly and evenly.

Complete grafting on the other side, joining 11 sts from back left side with 11 sts from back right side.

YARN CHOICES

Small: (not shown) Patons Fairytale Dreamtime 4ply Red 00091 and Hot Pink 02939

Medium: (not shown) Rowan Pure Wool Aran or any similar weight worsted/aran yarn

Large: Rowan Big Wool Sun 068

YOU WILL NEED

SMALL

41½yds (38m) of fingering-weight (4ply) yarn

1 set of 5 dpns size 1 (2.5mm)

2 sets of size 1 (2.5mm) circular needles

MEDIUM

104yds (95m) of worsted weight (Aran) yearn

1 set of 5 dpns size 8 (5mm)

2 sets of size 8 (5mm) circular needles

LARGE

149yds (136m) of bulky weight (chunky) yarn

1 set of 5 dpns size 15 (10mm)

2 sets of size 15 (10mm) circular needles

NOTIONS

Blunt-ended tapestry needle

Toy filling

Row counter

2 extra dpns for stitch holders

GAUGE (TENSION)

SMALL 30 sts x 41 rows to 4in (10cm) over st st

MEDIUM 18 sts x 25 rows to 4in (10cm) over st st

LARGE 7.5 sts x 10 rows to 4in (10cm) over st st

FINISHED SIZE (APPROX)

SMALL 5in x 5in (13cm x 13cm)

MEDIUM 8¾in x 8¾in (22cm x 22cm)

LARGE 17¾in x 17¾in (45cm x 45cm)

STAR: GET KNITTING

First side of star

Before you begin cut 5 lengths of yarn approx 4in (10cm) long for small size and 12in (30cm) for large size and set aside.

Begin with the centre of one side of star as folls:

*Cast on one st onto one dpn.

Row 1 (inc) K1, p1, k1 all into same st. (3 sts)

Row 2 P3.

Row 3 (inc) Kfb x 3. (6 sts)

Row 4 P6.

Row 5 (inc) Kfb x 6. (12 sts)

Divide sts onto 3 dpns or 2 circular ndls.

Join in the rnd.

Rnd 6 Knit. PM.

Rnd 7 (Kfb, k1) x 6. (18 sts)

Rnd 8 K18.

Rnd 9 (Kfb, k1) x 9. (27 sts)

Rnd 10 K27.

Rnd 11 (Kfb, k2) x 9. (36 sts)

Rnd 12 K36.

Rnd 13 (Kfb, k3) x 9. (45 sts)

Rnd 14 K45.

Rnd 15 (Kfb, k4) x 9. (54 sts)

Rnd 16 K54.

Rnd 17 (Kfb, k5) x 9. (63 sts)

Rnd 18 K63.

Rnd 19 (Kfb, k6) x 9. (72 sts)

Rnd 20 K72.

Rnd 21 (Kfb, k7) x 9. (81 sts)

Rnd 22 K81.

Rnd 23 (Kfb, k8) x 9. (90 sts)

Separate stitches

Separate sts to form bases for points as folls:

Thread tapestry ndl with one of the lengths of pre-cut yarn. Thread this through first 18 sts and set aside. Rep this process with rem 4 lengths of yarn (5 lengths of yarn with 18 sts on each).**

Second side of star

Work as for first side of star from * to **.

Star point one

Sl one set of 18 sts from one side of star onto dpn or circular ndl, sl one set of 18 sts from other side of star onto another dpn or circular ndl. Place WS's together and, holding dpns in left hand, rejoin yarn to sts and cont in rnds as folls:

Rnd 24 (dec) K1, skpo, k12, k2tog, k1, k1, skpo, k12, k2tog, k1. (32 sts)

Rnd 25 K32.

Rnd 26 (dec) K1, skpo, k10, k2tog, k1, k1, skpo, k10, k2tog, k1. (28 sts)

Rnd 27 K28.

Rnd 28 (dec) K1, skpo, k8, k2tog, k1, k1, skpo, k8, k2tog, k1. (24 sts)

Rnd 29 K24.

Rnd 30 (dec) K1, skpo, k6, k2tog, k1, k1, skpo, k6, k2tog, k1. (20 sts)

Rnd 31 K20.

Rnd 32 (dec) K1, skpo, k4, k2tog, k1, k1, skpo, k4, k2tog, k1. (16 sts)

Rnd 33 K16.

Rnd 34 (dec) K1, skpo, k2, k2tog, k1, k1, skpo, k2, k2tog, k1. (12 sts)

Rnd 35 K12.

Rnd 36 (dec) K1, skpo, k2tog, k1, k1, skpo, k2tog, k1. (8 sts)

Rnd 37 K8.

Rnd 38 (dec) Skpo, k2tog, skpo, k2tog. (4 sts)

Cut yarn. Thread tail end through rem sts, pull up to close and secure end.

Star points two, three and four

Work star points two, three and four as for star point one.

Stuff star firmly and evenly.

Star point five

Work as for star point one, stuffing the point a few rnds before the end. Ease the stuffing into the point with your fingers.

TO FINISH OFF

There may be gaps between the points and in the centre. If so, work some mattress stitches to close the hole. Work a stitch into the middle (through one side and out of the other) to keep the star flattish.

TECHNIQUES

FOR STRIPED LETTERS

Although many of the examples shown have been knitted in one colour, any of the letters can be knitted in stripes using the following method:

When you get to the end of one stripe, cut the yarn of the original colour, leaving a short tail end. This will be woven into the work later.

To add the new colour, leave a short tail end, hold it tight as you would hold the yarn to begin a regular row, and begin knitting. When you've finished knitting, weave all tail ends into the same colour stripe so that they stay distinct.

ABBREVIATIONS

All knitting patterns use abbreviations to save time and space. Below is a list of all the abbreviations used in the patterns for this book.

alt alternate

approx approximately

beg beginning

cm(s) centimetre(s)

cont continue

dpn double-pointed needle

dec decrease

DK double knitting

foll(s) follow(s)(ing)

g gram(s)

in(s) inch(es)

inc increase

k knit

k2tog knit the next two stitches together (decrease by one stitch)

kfb knit into front and back of the same stitch (increase by one stitch)

LH left hand

m meter

m1 make 1 stitch

mm millimetre(s)

ndl needle

oz ounce(s)

p purl

PM place marker

p2tog purl the next two stitches together (decrease by one stitch)

patt pattern

rem remain(ing)

rep repeat

rnd round

RH right hand

RS right side

skpo slip one, knit one, pass the slipped stitch over (decrease by one stitch)

sl slip

sl 1 slip one stitch

ssk slip, slip, knit (decrease by one stitch)

st(s) stitch(es)

st st stockinette stitch (stocking stitch)

tog together

w+t wrap and turn

WS wrong side

yds yards

BASIC EQUIPMENT

These patterns use double-pointed and circular needles, although for larger sized letters it may be easier to work directly onto circular needles. You will also need spare double-pointed needles and stitch holders for holding stitches, and markers to indicate the start of rounds. A large-eyed, blunt-ended darning or tapestry needle will be needed for sewing up. Use a good quality toy stuffing and, if you wish, a pair of tweezers for stuffing the narrower shapes.

YARNS

Each of the project instructions gives a generic description of the yarn that was used. The specific yarns I used are listed on the projects if you want to recreate the project exactly. Yarn companies frequently update their lines and may discontinue certain yarns or colours. If the yarns are not available, or if you want to use a substitute yarn, you will need to work out the yardage (meterage) needed, as yarns vary. Details will be on the ball band or on good yarn suppliers' websites so that you can make comparisons.

GAUGE

On the band or sleeve of every ball of yarn there is information on the gauge (what European knitters call 'tension') of the yarn. This tells you how many stitches and rows you should aim to achieve over 4in (10cm) square. The gauge differs depending on the needle size you use and the thickness of the yarn. However, we all knit differently. Some people are naturally loose knitters and others knit more tightly. The beauty about these projects is that the gauge doesn't really matter in most cases. If your letter is a little bit bigger or smaller than mine, who's to know!

CASTING ON

All projects start with getting the first stitches onto the knitting needles – in other words casting them on. These projects mainly use the Simple Sock Cast On Method.

Simple sock cast on method

Using one dpn cast on the given number of stitches:

1. *Hold needle with cast on stitches in your left hand and hold 2 empty dpns parallel in your right hand.

2. Slip first st purl-wise onto dpn closest to you, slip next st purl-wise onto dpn farthest away.**

Repeat step 2 until all the stitches are divided equally onto 2 parallel dpns, (eg, if casting on 28 sts you will end up with 14 sts on the front dpn and 14 sts on the back). Slide the sts to the other ends of the dpns, with yarn at back.

With right side facing, continue in rounds, beginning by knitting the stitches on the back dpn using a 3rd dpn to work the stitches.

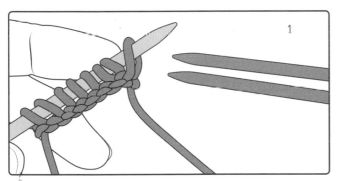

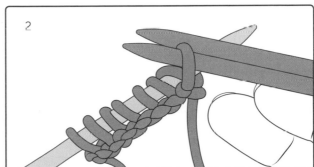

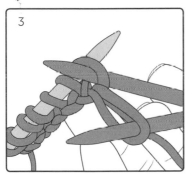

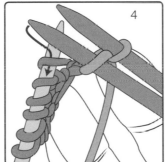

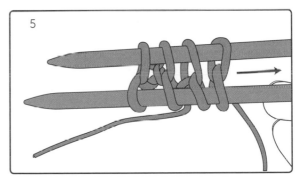

Backward loop method

This is the best cast-on method when adding stitches in the middle of a row.

1. Hold the working yarn in your left hand with the needle in your right. Extend your left index finger parallel to the yarn, dip your finger under the yarn and pull it towards you.

2. Move the tip of the needle from the base of your finger so that the needle is through the loop with your finger. Remove your finger and tighten the loop on the needle.

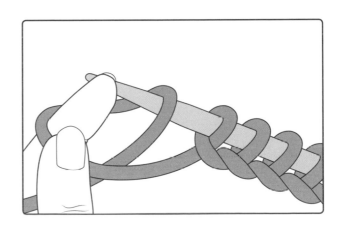

THE KNIT STITCH

Knit stitch is the most basic stitch in knitting. It can be used completely on its own, when knitting in the round or to produce stockinette stitch (stocking stitch). When it is used on its own for working back and forth along rows, it produces garter stitch.

1. The working stitches will be on the left-hand needle. Take the right-hand needle and insert the tip from right to left into the first loop on the left-hand needle.

2. Wrap the yarn from back to front around the tip of the right-hand needle.

3. Slide the needle down to catch this new loop of yarn. Slip the loop off the left-hand needle and onto the right-hand needle. This is your first stitch. Repeat the process until all the stitches have been knitted off the left-hand needle onto the right-hand one.

THE PURL STITCH

The purl stitch is the perfect complement to the knit stitch. The right side of each looks like the reverse side of the other. If purl stitch is used when working back and forth, alternating rows with knit stitch, the combination produces stockinette stitch (stocking stitch).

1. The working stitches will be on your left-hand needle.

2. Wrap the yarn counterclockwise around the tip of the right-hand needle.

3. Use the tip of the right-hand needle to pick up the new loop of yarn. Slide the loop off the left-hand needle onto the right-hand needle. This is your first stitch. Repeat until all stitches have been knitted off the left-hand needle onto the right-hand one.

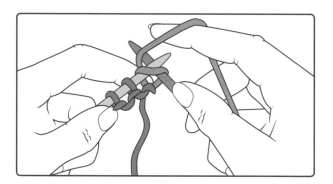

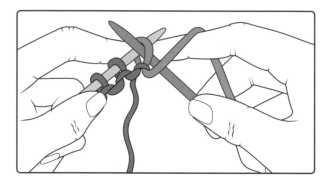

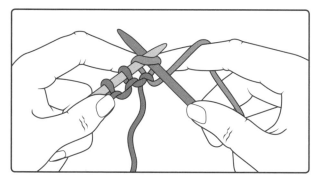

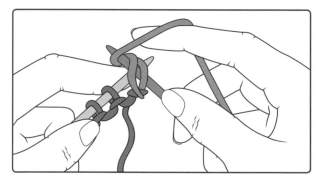

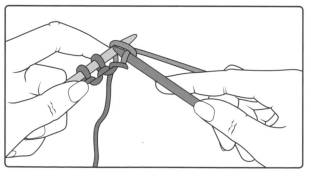

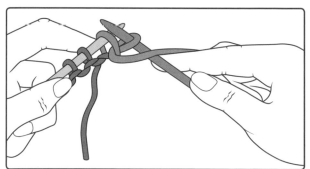

BASIC STITCH PATTERNS

Only the very basic stitch patterns are used to make the projects in this book. They are mostly knitted in stockinette stitch (also referred to as stocking stitch by Europeans). When working stockinette stitch in rounds you knit every round. When working the short row sections you work one row knit, the next row purl.

BINDING OFF

Binding off (also referred to as 'casting off' by Europeans) is what you do to remove the stitches from the needle without them unravelling. Below are instructions for the standard binding-off of one edge. Most of the projects also use Kitchener stitch (grafting).

Standard bind off

1. Work the first stitch on the left-hand needle as if making a regular knit stitch. Then knit the second stitch. Insert the left-hand needle into the first stitch on the right-hand needle.

2. Pass this stitch over the second loop on the right-hand needle and drop it off the needle. This makes the first bound-off stitch. To continue, knit the next stitch. Use your left-hand needle to pass the new first stitch over the second stitch and drop it off the needle. Carry on until all the stitches in the row have been bound off.

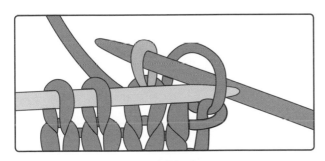

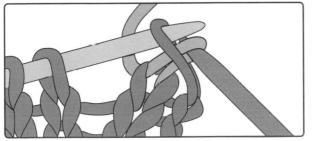

Kitchener stitch

1. Thread your tapestry needle with the tail of yarn. Insert your tapestry needle into the first stitch on the front needle as if you were going to purl, pull the yarn through and leave the stitch on the needle.

2. Now insert your tapestry needle into the first stitch on the back needle as if you were going to knit, pull the yarn through and leave the stitch on the needle.

These first two steps are set-up steps and will only be done once during the process.

3. Insert tapestry ndl into first st on front ndl as if you were going to knit, pull yarn through and let that st drop off ndl.

4. Insert tapestry ndl into next st on front ndl as if you were going to purl, pull yarn through but don't let it drop off ndl.

5. Insert tapestry ndl into next st on back ndl as if you were going to purl, pull yarn through and let that st drop off ndl.

6. Insert ndl into next st on back ndl as if you were going to knit, pull yarn through but don't let it drop off ndl.

Rep steps 3–6 until all sts have been joined.

To avoid 'pointy' corners start your Kitchener stitch by working 2 sts from the front and 2 sts from the back. Then continue with just one st from the front and one st from the back until you reach the end and work the last 2 sts on the front and the last 2 sts on the back together.

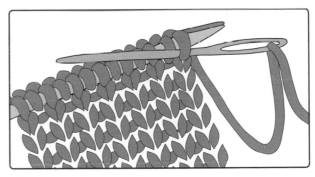

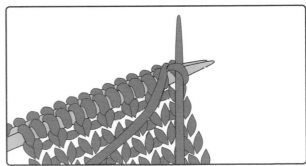

SHAPING

The different shaping techniques you will need are explained below.

Decreasing stitches

Decreasing stitches is where you lose stitches, in these patterns usually one at a time. This can be achieved in several ways.

K2TOG (knit two stitches together)

Knit through the next two stitches as though they were one stitch. This decreases by one stitch and the decrease will appear as if lying in a direction from left to right.

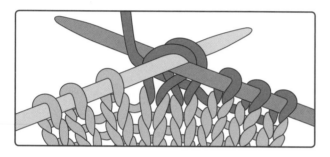

SKPO
(slip one, knit one, pass slipped stitch over)

Slip the next stitch, knit the following stitch then pick up the slipped stitch with the left-hand needle and pass it over the top of the stitch just knitted. This will decrease by one stitch and the decrease will appear as if lying in a direction from right to left.

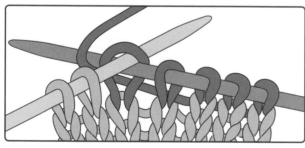

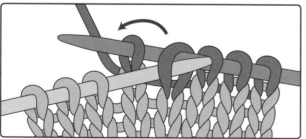

P2TOG (purl two stitches together)

Purl through the next two stitches as though they were one stitch. This decreases by one stitch.

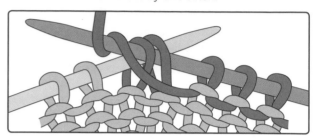

Increasing stitches

Increasing stitches is where you make a stitch.

KFB (knit into the front and back)

Knit into the front of the next stitch on the left-hand needle. Instead of removing it from the needle, knit into it again through the back loop. Then slip the original stitch off the left-hand needle.

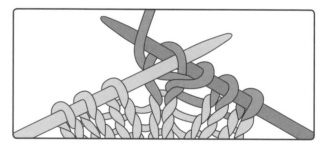

M1 (make one stitch)

With the right-hand needle pick up the loop lying between the two needles and place it onto the left-hand needle. Then with the right-hand needle knit into the back of this loop and let it drop off the left-hand needle. This creates an invisible increase of one stitch.

SHORT ROW SHAPING

Working short rows is a simple and very effective way of shaping your work. On each row you work one less stitch and on the final row you work across all the stitches. Short row shapings uses the wrap and turn (w+t) technique.

W+T (wrap and turn)

w&t on k rows take yarn between ndls to front, sl next st from LH ndl to RH ndl p-wise, take yarn between ndls to back, sl the st back to LH ndl. Turn.

w&t on p rows take yarn between ndls to back, sl next st from LH ndl to RH ndl p-wise, take yarn between ndls to front, sl the st back to LH ndl. Turn.

KNITTING IN THE ROUND

All of the projects in this book are knitted in the round on double-pointed needles. Knitting in this way is great because it saves you having to sew up fiddly seams later.

The rounds are numbered straight on from any preceding row or round, although sometimes you need to knit part of a round to get to the correct place to start knitting the next part of your letter.

Knitting on double-pointed needles

Double-pointed needles (dpn) are shorter than standard needles and easier to handle than a circular needle when you have only a few stitches to work in the round on.

1. Cast on as normal and distribute the stitches equally over three double-pointed needles.

2. Continue knitting round, transferring the stitches so you have an equal number of stitches on each needle.

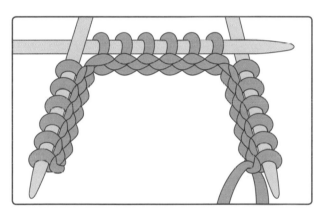

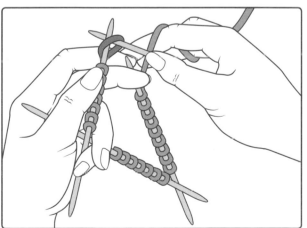

MAKING UP

There are various ways of sewing up knitting, so use whichever you like or suits the occasion best. Always use the same yarn you knitted with so the stitches are less visible. Often you will be able to use the long end you left when you cast on. It's best to use a darning or tapestry needle with a large eye and blunt end so that you don't split the yarn.

Weaving in ends

You will have some loose yarn ends from casting on and binding off, so weave these in first. One of the best ways to weave in the loose ends so they will be invisible is to thread the yarn end through a darning needle and sew it into the seam by passing the needle through the 'bumps' of the stitches on the wrong side of the work. Sew them in for 1–2in (2.5–5cm) and then snip off any excess yarn.

Mattress stitch

Put the two pieces of knitting next to each other, knit sides up and seams matching. Run the yarn through the centre of the first stitch on one piece of knitting, then down through the centre of the first stitch on the other piece of knitting. Next go through the second stitch on the first piece of knitting and down through the centre of the second stitch on the other piece. Continue in this way along the row, pulling up the stitches fairly tightly.

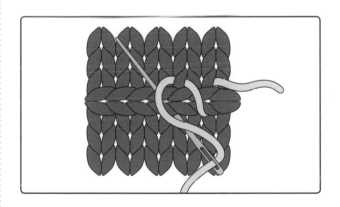

Stuffing your letters

Toy stuffing is an essential component for your knitted letters. You will be able to find a suitable brand at haberdashery and craft stores. Use stuffing that is specifically designed for toys so you can be sure it is safe for children. Check the safety logo before you buy it.

Stuff the letters fairly firmly and evenly, adding enough stuffing to give it shape (refer to photographs for the final shape), but at the same time taking care not to overstuff. If you overstuff, the knitted fabric will stretch too far, the rows will look crooked, you will see stuffing through the stitches and your letter will look lumpy.

When you're finished, gently massage the letter into just the right shape. If it's a bit lumpy, massage those lumps until they loosen up and redistribute a bit. If a part of the letter is sagging, tug it into place. Smooth the knitted rows into place. Don't be afraid to work with your finished letters to make them look their very best.

ADDING EXTRA SUPPORT

For some of the larger letters in particular you may find them a bit too floppy for display purposes, especially if a soft yarn has been used. To combat this add strips of thick sturdy card (about half the width and a little less than the length of the section that needs support) inside the letter before stuffing, and then stuff around the strips. These strips can also be gently bent to add support to curved areas.

BLOCKING

This is another shaping option to try, although it works better with smaller and medium letters. After stuffing, spray the letter all over with warm water until the letter is lightly misted (not soaking) and then re-shape and massage to shape. Do this gently as too much agitation may cause the letter to felt.

Sewing in final ends

Once you have stuffed the letters, you will need to close the small opening in the middle of the seam. I knot together the two ends of the yarn used for sewing the seams, then thread the ends through the letter so that the knot is hidden and the ends are kept long. Don't cut the ends too short or the knot may come undone.

SUPPLIERS

Patons
www.coatscrafts.co.uk

Patons (USA/CAN)
320 Livingstone Avenue South
Listowel, ON, Canada, N4W 3H3
Tel: +1 888 368 8401
email: inquire@patonsyarns.com
www.patonsyarns.com

Coats Crafts UK
PO Box 22, Lingfield House
Lingfield Point, McMullen Road
Darlington DL1 1YJ
Tel: +44 (0)1325 394237
email: consumer.ccuk@coats.com
www.coatscrafts.co.uk

Patons (AUS)
PO Box 7276, Melbourne Victoria 3004
Tel: +61 (0)3 9380 3888
email: enquiries@auspinners.com.au
www.patons.biz

Rowan (including RYC) (USA)
www.knitrowan.com
(USA) Westminster Fibers Inc
165 Ledge Street, Nashua
New Hampshire 03060
Tel: +1 603 886 5041/5043
email: info@westminsterfibers.com
www.westminsterfibers.com
Rowan (UK)
Green Lane Mill, Holmfirth HD9 2DX
Tel: +44 (0)1484 681881
email: info@knitrowan.com
www.knitrowan.com
Australian Country Spinners Pty Ltd (AUS)
Level 7, 409 St Kilda Road
Melbourne, Victoria 3004
Tel: +61 (0)3 9380 3888
email: tkohut@auspinners.com.au
www. auspinners.com.au

Stitch Craft Create (UK)
Brunel House, Forde Close,
Newton Abbott, Devon, TQ12 4PU
www.stitchcraftcreate.co.uk

Martha Pullen
149 Old Big Cove Road
Brownsboro, AL 35741
www.marthapullen.com

ACKNOWLEDGMENTS

Many thanks are due to Jeni Hennah, Matt Hutchings, Lin Clements and Rachel Vowles and all the team at D&C for your patience, advice, good ideas and knowledge. Very grateful thanks also to Stitch Craft Create for providing all the yarns etc!

ABOUT THE AUTHOR

Claire Garland's early memories of deliberating over her favourite toy-making book as a seven-year old, before cutting and sticking wondrous creations and designing clothes for her teenage dolls, live on in the toys she designs today.

The grown-up Claire studied art and design in Cardiff, Wales, and a year after finishing started designing needlepoint kits for the internationally renowned company Primavera.

For her own young children, Claire first tried her hand at embroidering bed linen before rekindling her interest in knitting. The knitted dolls she designed, with their characterful looks and fashionable clothes, captured the imagination of many so much that their own special blogger website was created.

Today Claire lives with her husband and three children (and no real, only knitted, pets) in a pretty cottage in Cornwall where she writes and illustrates her books on sewing, knitting and crochet, makes toys and runs her online mail order company www.dotpebbles.com for her own brand knitted doll kits.

INDEX

A DAVID & CHARLES BOOK
© F&W Media International, Ltd 2013

David & Charles is an imprint of F&W Media International, Ltd
Brunel House, Forde Close, Newton Abbot, TQ12 4PU, UK

F&W Media International, Ltd is a subsidiary of F+W Media, Inc
10151 Carver Road, Suite #200, Blue Ash, OH 45242, USA

Text and Designs © Claire Garland 2013
Layout and Photography © F&W Media International, Ltd 2013

First published in the UK and USA in 2013

ISBN-13: 978-1-4463-0381-8 paperback
ISBN-10: 1-4463-0381-0 paperback

Printed in China by RR Donnelley for:
F&W Media International, Ltd
Brunel House, Forde Close, Newton Abbot, TQ12 4PU, UK

10 9 8 7 6 5 4 3 2 1

Acquisitions Editor: Jeni Hennah
Desk Editor: Matthew Hutchings
Project Editor: Lin Clements and Rachel Vowles
Art Editor: Anna Fazakerley
Photographer: Jack Gorman
Production Controller: Kelly Smith

F+W Media publishes high quality books on a wide range of subjects.
For more great book ideas visit: www.stitchcraftcreate.co.uk